EASING INTO JAZZ

Jazz Originals & Improvisations
To Standard Changes

By Noreen Lienhard

USA: musicbooksnow.com
Europe: goodmusic.co.uk

CONTENTS

———

Easing Into Jazz is published by Ekay Music Inc., Bedford Hills, New York 10507

Editor-in-chief: Edward Shanaphy
Project Coordinator: Stuart Isacoff
Design and Production by Anita J. Tumminelli
Cover Design by Loraine Machlin

Distributed by Alfred Publications, Inc.
and Ekay Music Inc.

USA: musicbooksnow.com/steinway
Europe: goodmusic.co.uk/steinway

A NOTE ABOUT 'LAY-FLAT' BINDING

This special binding is designed to keep your music book open on the music stand. It will need a slight preparation on your part to help accomplish this. Place the book on a clean, flat surface and open it to a section near the front. With the heel of your hand, apply a gentle but firm pressure at various spots along the spine where the pages meet. Do not strike at the spine, and do not run your hand or thumb along the spine. This could cause the pages to wrinkle. Repeat this pressing process at various places throughout the book to break it in. When you have selected a piece to play, repeat the process again for that piece, and you may also, at this point, fold the book back on itself gently squeezing the binding.

PURPOSE

Easing Into Jazz has been created to guide the intermediate to advanced piano student in the fundamentals of improvisation. By utilizing well-known chord progressions of popular standards—ones that are particular favorites of jazz professionals—and creating new tunes and improvisations for those progressions, this book is of significant value to the student musician for gaining insight into how an improvisation is constructed. These new melodies and jazz lines for existing progressions (known as "contrafacts") also serve to supply the student with instant improvisations, perfect for incorporating into one's own repertoire without a great deal of difficulty, while still sounding highly polished.

Many jazz giants have used this technique of creating new jazz tunes based on the progressions of well-known standards. Horace Silver wrote such tunes as Quicksilver, May-Reh, and Split Kick to the chords of Lover Come Back To Me, All God's Chillun Got Rhythm, and There Will Never Be Another You, respectively. Miles Davis wrote Dig to the progression of Sweet Georgia Brown; Charlie Parker wrote Donna Lee to (Back Home Again In) Indiana, as well as a host of others, including Hot House, Bird Of Paradise and Quasimodo, to the chords of What Is This Thing Called Love, All The Things You Are, and Embraceable You. Literally thousands of jazz musicians have learned their art, in great part, by getting such improvised tunes into their repertoire, and learning to extend the improvisations in their own way.

The new tunes and improvisations contained in this volume correspond generally to chord progressions for the ten standards listed below, and while they are not exactly the "as written" ones for the standards, they are similar to those used frequently by jazz pianists:

Past Tense (*Yesterdays*)
Castles In The Air (*Imagination*)
Romantic Etude (*In A Sentimental Mood*)
Dança Verão (*Summer Samba*)
Sea And Sand (*Wave*)
Starry-Eyed (*Isn't It Romantic*)
Night Wishes (*Darn That Dream*)
Surprise Encounter (*Have You Met Miss Jones?*)
Vintage Charm (*I'm Old Fashioned*)
Waiting For Mr. Right (*Someday My Prince Will Come*)

The pieces are constructed so that the first chorus, the melody of the tune, can be used as a quieter improvisation to the standard, while the second chorus represents a more complex solo. Jazz solos are often built that way, starting simply and then growing in tension and complexity. — E.S.

FROM THE AUTHOR

A heartfelt "thank you" to my talented and insightful editor, Edward Shanaphy, for creating the "Purpose" to this text. Because he has covered everything so completely, there is nothing more to add, other than a brief personal commentary:

The study of jazz is a lifetime journey filled with challenges and goals, growth and discovery. It is my hope that all who play these pieces will use them as a stepping-stone to further their own musical development. After learning these "contrafacts" and familiarizing yourself with the standards upon which they are based, please feel free to take liberties with them. Embellish the melodies and rhythms, reharmonize the progressions, change the accompaniments, and create your own improvisations, introductions, and endings. Be spontaneous…the possibilities are endless. As you "journey" through this book, read the introductions to them in the "About The Music" section. These target some "points of interest." The rest are yours to discover.

ABOUT THE MUSIC

Past Tense (based on "Yesterdays"): This is one of my favorite progressions for improvisation, because the key centers are so accessible. D minor is a popular key for many standards, so this is an excellent chord pattern with which to become familiar.

POINTS OF INTEREST:

This piece has an "all-purpose" introduction, consisting of alternating measures of Dm and Eb7, which also double as a fade-out vamp ending.

At letter A (m.6), the melody is set to a bass line with a free and easy "2" feel. Because the melody in the B section (m.22) is nearly identical, intensity and momentum are created by changing the left hand to a traditional 4/4 "walking" bass line.

In the solo section (A, m.38), the left hand treatment consists of bass notes and rhythmically punctuated intervals. Melodic sequencing is illustrated in the right hand improvisation from measure 46-50.

Measures 62-66 of B make use of a tritone triad technique, with the improvisation consisting of notes from both the primary chord and its tritone substitution (A7/Eb, D7/Ab, G7/Db, C7/Gb, F7/B).

Castles in the Air (based on "Imagination"): I learned the original version of this tune from my father, a talented saxophonist I credit with encouraging me to develop a large repertoire of standards; they have served me well to this day.

POINTS OF INTEREST:

This tune is in a 36-bar irregular form: the last A section consists of twelve measures, instead of eight. The introduction consists of ascending scale tone sevenths in Eb, over a Bb pedal point.

The solo at A1 (m.36), features a variety of rhythmic figures: 8th note triplets, 16th notes, and quarter note triplets, supported by a modified stride ballad treatment in the left hand.

In measure 53 (letter B), a descending diminished scale (alternation of whole and half steps) is used over the ii7-V7 progression (Am7-D7).

The coda (m.72) begins on the flat five (A), of the home

key (Eb) and descends chromatically, via various chord qualities, until the Ebmaj7 resolution. This is a "must learn" ending with countless applications.

Romantic Etude (based on "In A Sentimental Mood"): This lovely harmonic progression offers some challenging key centers during the B section, but it is still very playable. The left hand treatment throughout is primarily a "modified stride" technique, involving changes of hand position and extensive use of the pedal to sustain the roots.

POINTS OF INTEREST:

Improvisation based on polychords occurs during the A2 section (measure 39-43). The right hand arpeggio is based on the harmony a whole step above the left hand chord (Em/Dm7, Am/Gm7).

This technique continues in measures 44-45, using *tritone* triads, chords whose roots are a tritone (augmented fourth or diminished fifth) apart (Ab/D7, Db/G7, Gb/C7). (To find a tritone, simply play three whole steps. From C, for example, play D, E and F# and you have arrived at the tritone interval between C and F#.)

Both A3 sections (melody m.23, solo m.55) make use of substitute harmonies commonly used by professional jazz musicians. The progression begins with the half-diminished

7th chord built on the flat fifth (B) of the home key (F) and descends chromatically to the target chord (Dm), which is the relative minor of the home key. This harmonic device adds a fresh twist to the structure and can be used in many tunes.

The coda is an extended ending, which delays the resolution to the final chord for two measures. The chords descend chromatically, until Gb6 is introduced as a tritone substitution for C7, thus leading to the F (add 2).

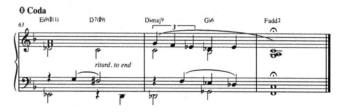

Dança Verão (based on "Summer Samba"): The original model for this contrafact has always been one of my favorites but it is not one I've often been called upon to perform, so I was delighted to have the opportunity to work with this progression—a great ii-V workout in a friendly key.

POINTS OF INTEREST:

The vamp introduction doubles as a fade out ending, constructed on I, IV, I, and bII chords.

This piece contains a great deal of syncopation in both hands; this is essential in a solo piano setting, where there are no supporting instruments (bass and drums), to help establish the Latin groove. Remember to play the eighth notes with a "straight" feel.

Notable in the solo is the exchange between the harmonized melody and the bass line from measures 43-50.

The right hand in measures 51-54 (harmonized in thirds) presents quarter note triplets against the already familiar left hand rhythm. Blending these two will take a little practice.

Sea and Sand (based on "Wave"): This was the first piece written for the book, completed before the Jamaican vacation that inspired the title. Set in the key of D, it is an opportunity to depart from the C, F, Bb, and Eb key centers we play in so often. The parallel minor chord (Dm) is also prominent in the progression.

POINTS OF INTEREST:

The repeated vamp introduction with its ii-V movement can be used in virtually any tune, and in any style. Experiment using it with some of the pieces in your repertoire.

The Bossa Nova feel is achieved by emphasizing syncopation in both hands. In this style the eighth notes are played "straight" instead of with a swing lilt. In measures 5-9, the left hand plays a chord root on beat one, with the rest of the chord entering on the "and" of beat two.

Notice how the right hand melody contains many tied eighth notes, which emphasize the "and" (weaker) part of the beat. Later on, the right hand makes use of quarter note triplet rhythms (m.11-13). Similar rhythmic devices are used throughout.

In measures 63-69 (letter B) of the solo, the melody has been harmonized in sixths. This open harmonization is very compatible with the Bossa style; it also functions as a departure from single line melodies.

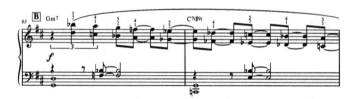

The coda is an extended triple tag ending starting on a Bb13 (the VI of D minor).

On the third repetition (m.89), a series of dominant chords descends chromatically to the end. Measure 93 and 94 incorporate bluesy fills, before coming to rest on D(add9).

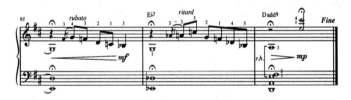

Starry-Eyed (based on "Isn't It Romantic"): I have a special arrangement when I play the original of this contrafact, so I really enjoyed doing something completely different with it this time around.

POINTS OF INTEREST:

The introduction is set up with a Bb pedal point beneath the right hand line. The same device is used as a solo break in measures 27 and 28. Notice that the pedal point is the V of the home key (Eb).

When the melody begins at letter A, the left hand half note intervals provide a "two feel" until more syncopated figures are introduced in the first ending (letter B, m.13). Throughout the tune, the swing feel remains strong, despite the absence of a steady 4/4 walking bass.

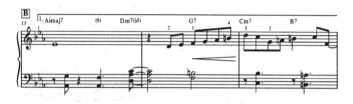

The most notable part of this arrangement is the unison octave treatment in the solo section, beginning at measure 45. This style is the trademark of great players like Oscar Petersen and Phineas Newborn. Between phrases, some punctuated chords are added, as in measures 48, 51, 52, and 53.

To get a better grasp on this technique, practice two-handed scales to get completely comfortable with finger patterns in all keys. Then play 8th note melodies and improvisations in octaves to gain agility and work out finger issues.

Night Wishes (based on "Darn That Dream"): The late Sal Salvador (guitarist with Stan Kenton) favored the original of this contrafact.

I was fortunate to have performed it with him many times, and was very pleased when it was chosen for this project. G major is also a refreshing change from the flat key signatures of most standards.

POINTS OF INTEREST:

The introduction utilizes another chord progression with many applications. Starting on the iii (B), the first two measures descend by whole steps in ii-V fashion. The next two measures begin a totally chromatic descent starting on F7(b5). Notice that this chord is a tritone substitution (by root) of the Bm7(b5) in measure one. The same relationship is seen between the first chords of measures two and four (Am7 and Eb7(b5), respectively).

The most notable feature of this piece is the B section of the solo. Measures 47-54 feature block chords (or "locked hands"), a style synonymous with George Shearing. The melody is doubled an octave below, and the other chord tones fill in the harmony between them. This is another "must learn" technique, to add variety and charm to your arrangements.

The coda (m.63) is an extended ending, seven measures beyond the original form. Measure 69 could have resolved to the final chord, but instead, its tritone substitution (Db) was chosen to begin a chromatic descent and delayed resolution to Gmaj9.

Surprise Encounter (based on "Have You Met Miss Jones"): I wanted to include this tune because the bridge contains some difficult key centers, a challenge to which every pianist should be exposed. The rest of the tune, with its F key center, is quite manageable. This progression is loads of fun to play, as soon as a "comfort zone" is reached.

POINTS OF INTEREST:

This piece contains an all-purpose introduction, beginning on the iii chord and descending chromatically to the I. Depending on the desired sound, the dominant chords in measure two and four can be changed to minor 7ths.

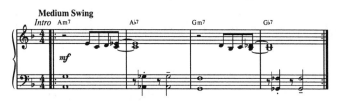

Throughout the arrangement, left hand bass notes and syncopated intervals facilitate the swing feel. Much of the left hand syncopation focuses on the "and" of two, as in measures 10, 11, 14 and 15. To create a little twist, in measures 53-54 the device has been reversed, with the interval preceding the bass note, and the syncopation occurring on the "and" of one.

Melodic sequencing is used in measures 19-20 and 21-22 during the B section of the melody, and again during the solo in measures 46-47. Try practicing this idea of creating a sequence while improvising in other contexts.

The coda (m.64) features a triple tag ending based on harmonic material from the introduction. (After comparing the two, play the introduction using the chords in measures 65 and 66.)

The sharp nine chord at the end is a popular way to conclude jazz pieces.

Vintage Charm (based on "I'm Old Fashioned"): Many jazz greats have improvised on this structure, which presents numerous opportunities for harmonic and rhythmic variation.

POINTS OF INTEREST:

This tune has an interesting area where the chords move scale-wise as the qualities change. Look at measures 25 through 28 and 61 through 64. Challenging to improvise on AND challenging to compose a new melody over!!

The introduction features a C pedal point with arpeggiated augmented triads descending in whole steps. A favorite pattern of Thelonious Monk, this is used again as a solo break in measure 39-40, and in measure 76 before the D.S. These triads are derived from the whole tone scale: C, D, E, F#, G#, A# C.

A left hand walking bass (beginning m.5) provides a swinging momentum and a solid foundation for the melody. This treatment alternates with the use of roots and rhythmic intervals, as shown at letter B (m.13). In measure 41, at the beginning of the solo, a "two feel" (half note) bass line is used.

Also notable is rhythmic displacement of the melody. The same melodic phrase is placed at different points in consecutive measures; this is another Monk technique. It occurs in measures 13-16, and again during the solo in measures 61 and 62.

Waiting for Mr. Right (based on "Someday My Prince Will Come"): The original model for this contrafact is undoubtedly one of the most popular jazz waltzes of all time, so it was a "must include" in this book.

POINTS OF INTEREST:

The introduction, which also doubles as a fade out ending, features a left hand C pedal point below the right hand harmonies.

Momentum for the jazz waltz feel is supplied through the equal dotted quarter note division of the measure, as seen in the left hand of the introduction. When the treatment involves intervals rather than single bass notes, such as in measures 5, 6, and 8, there is still an entrance on the "and" of two, to split the measure rhythmically in half. With the feel established, the melody and improvisation can freely float above.

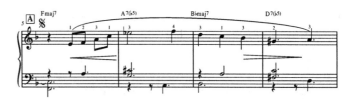

I always think of Bill Evans when working with this progression. When playing in 3/4, he often used duples in the right hand to create interesting rhythmic effects. This is illustrated in bars 11, 27, 45, 59, 64, and 66.

Also notable are measures 57-60, where harmony in thirds breaks up the single line right hand.

THE
MUSIC

PAST TENSE

Noreen Lienhard

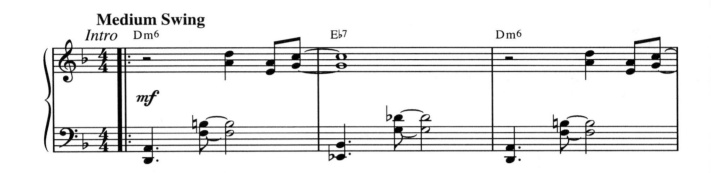

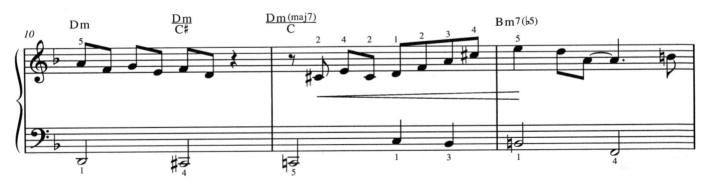

Copyright © 2007 Ekay Music, Inc.

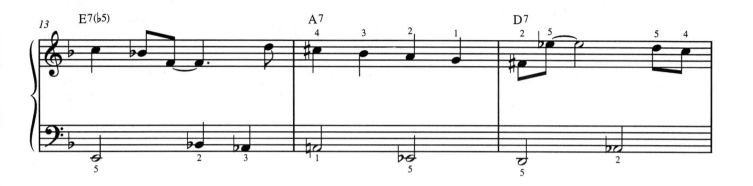

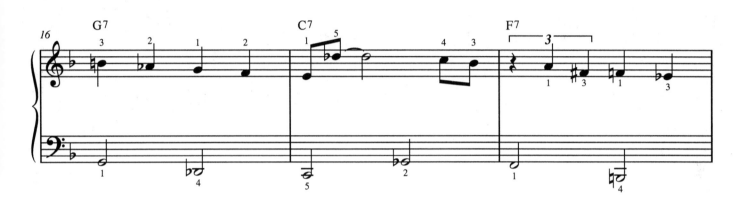

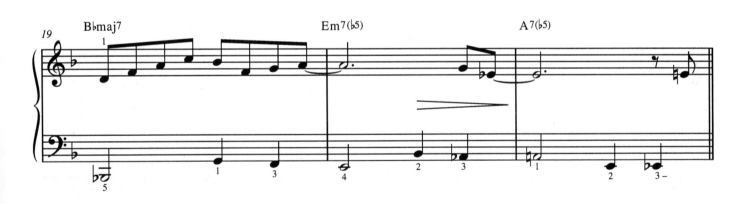

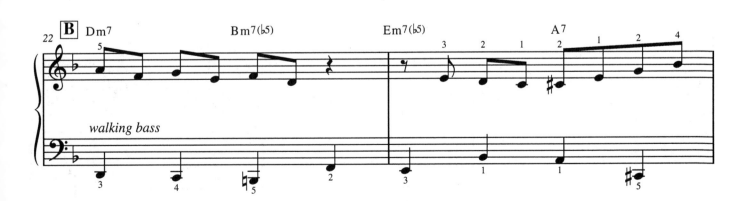

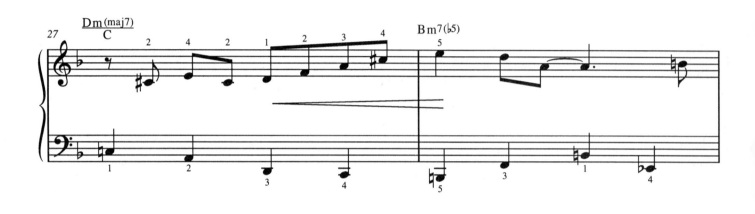

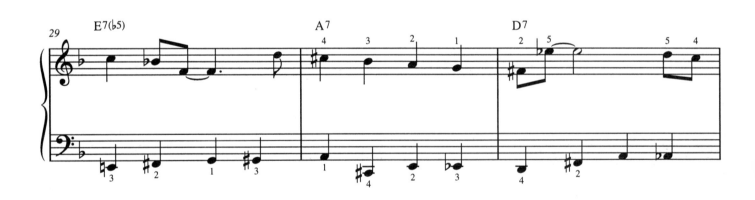

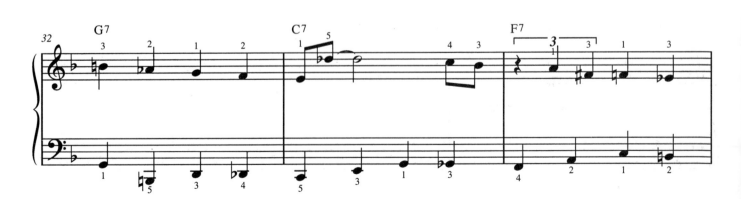

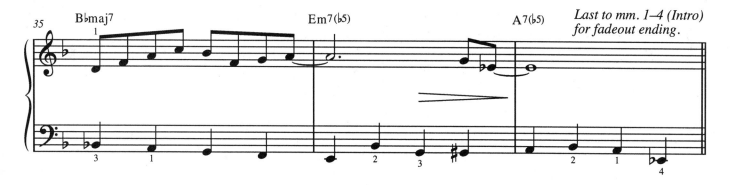

Last to mm. 1–4 (Intro) for fadeout ending.

A *Solo*

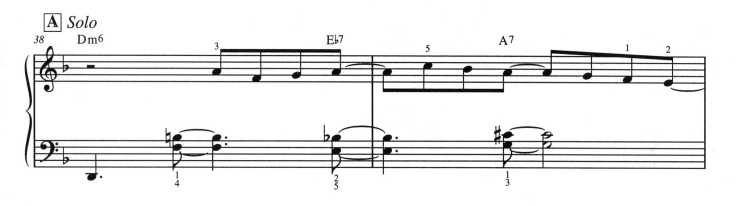

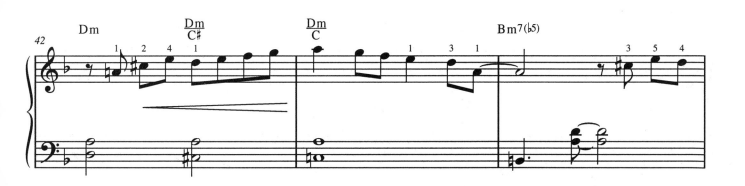

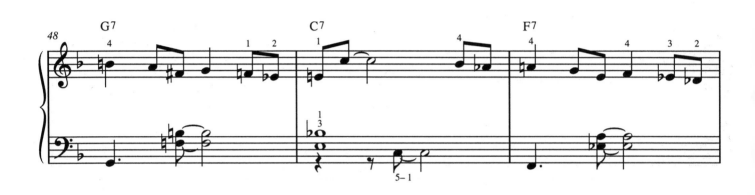

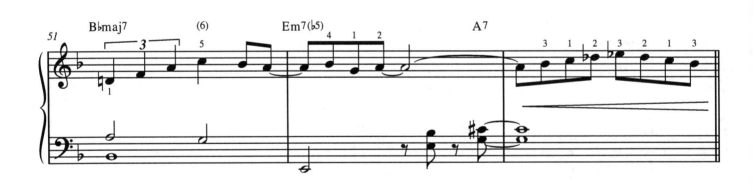

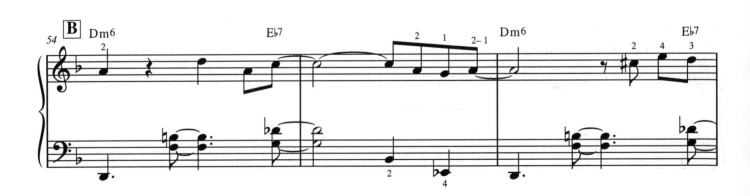

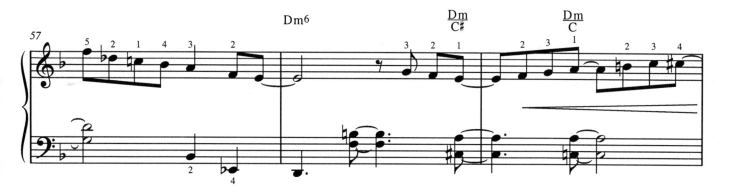

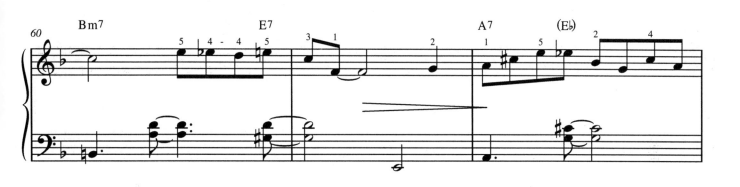

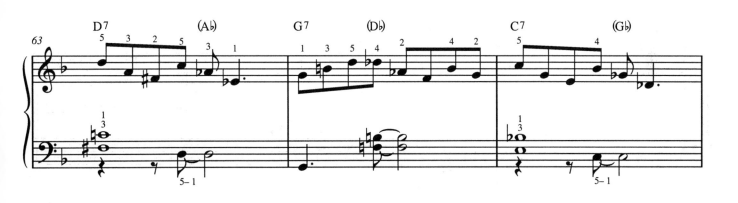

CASTLES IN THE AIR

Noreen Lienhard

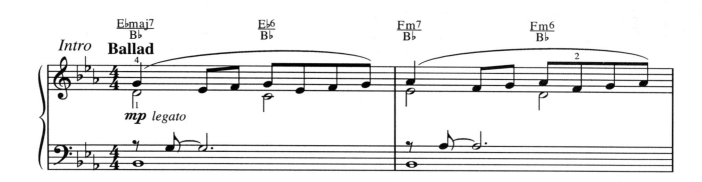

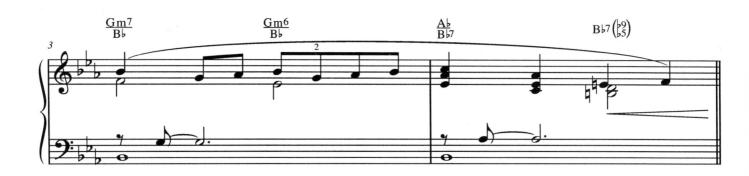

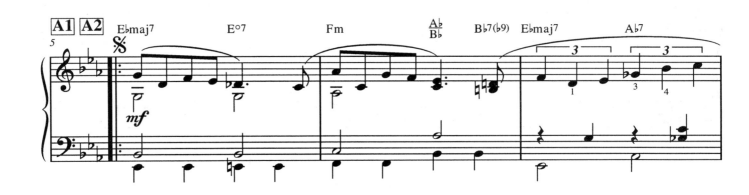

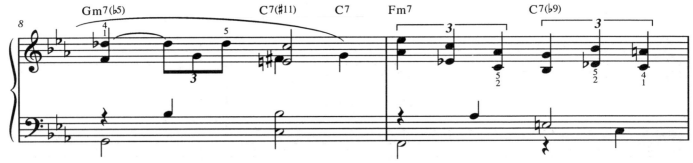

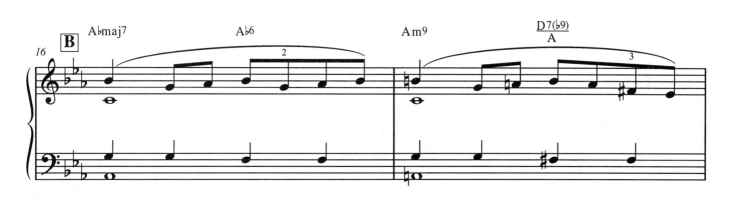

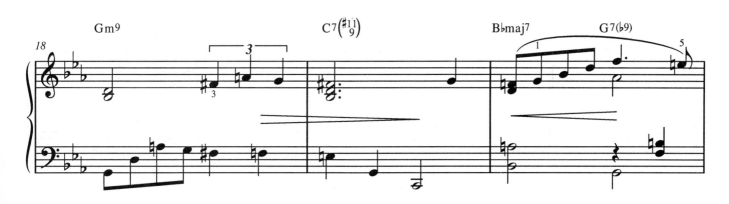

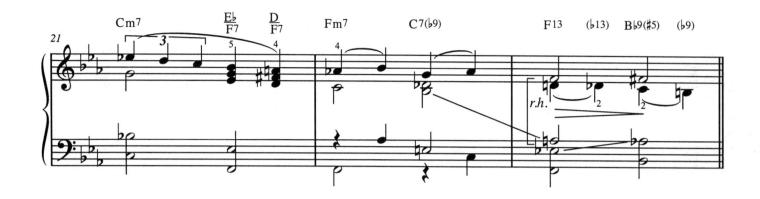

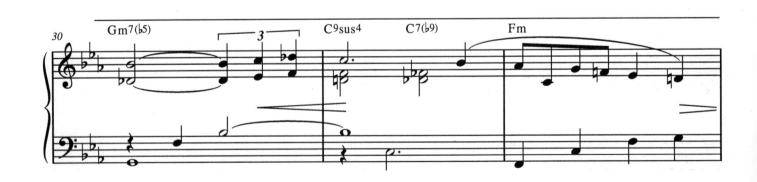

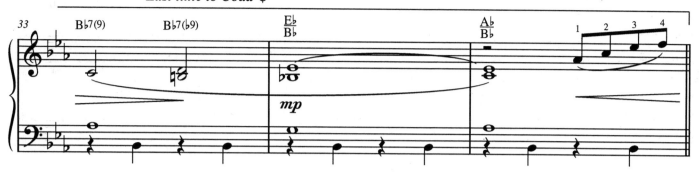

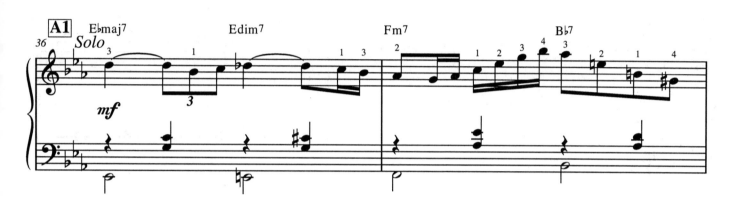

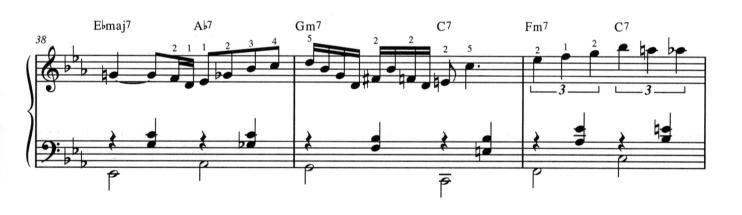

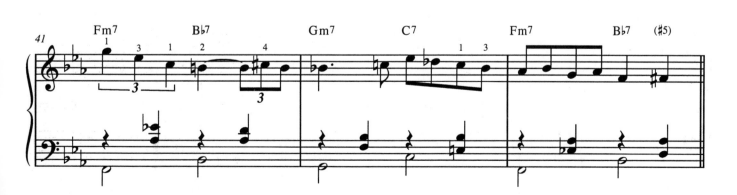

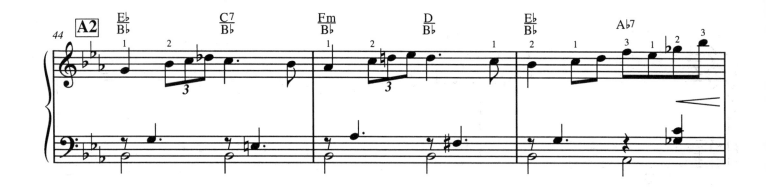

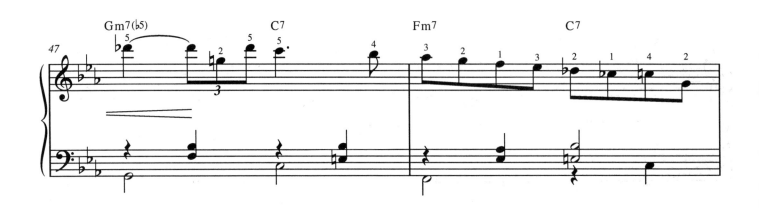

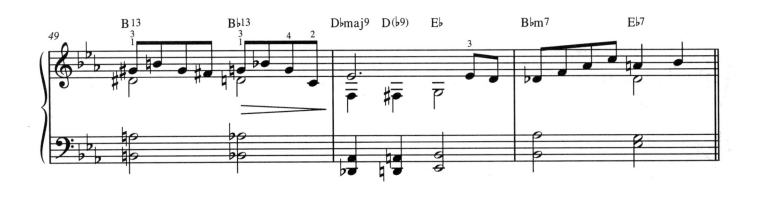

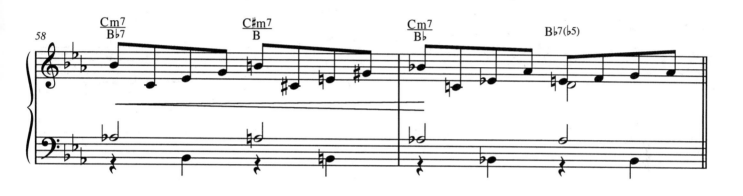

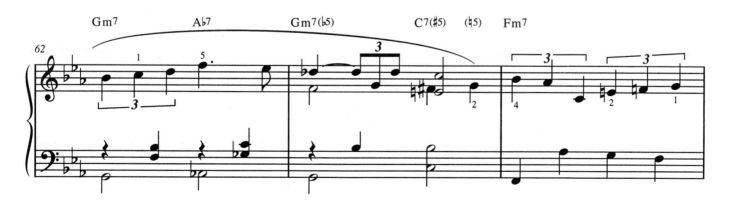

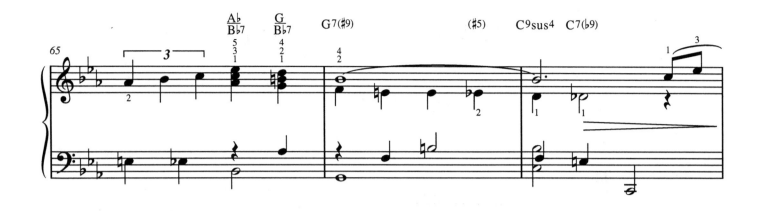

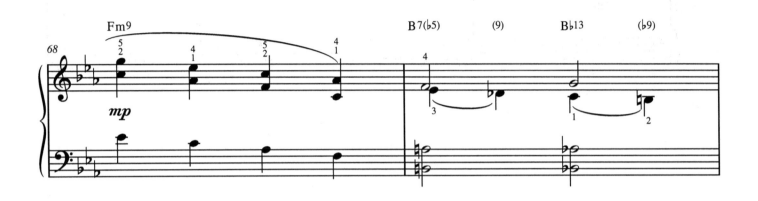

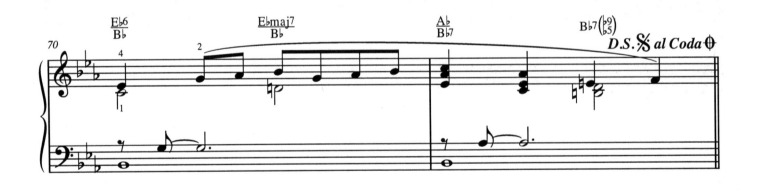

ROMANTIC ETUDE

Noreen Lienhard

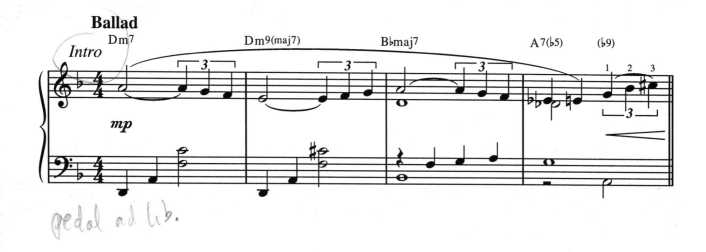

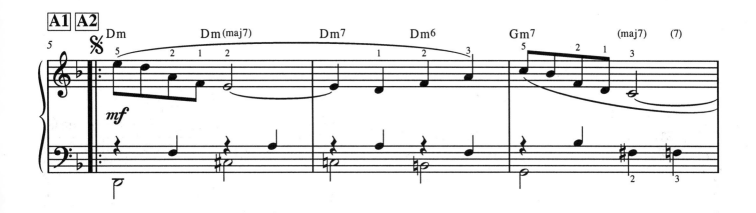

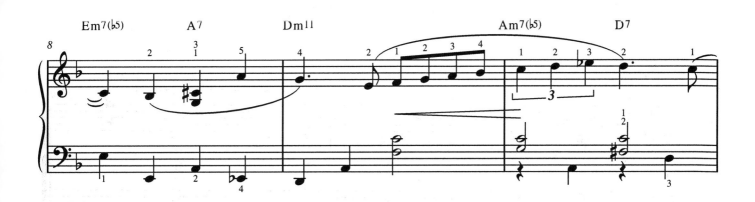

Copyright © 2007 Ekay Music, Inc.

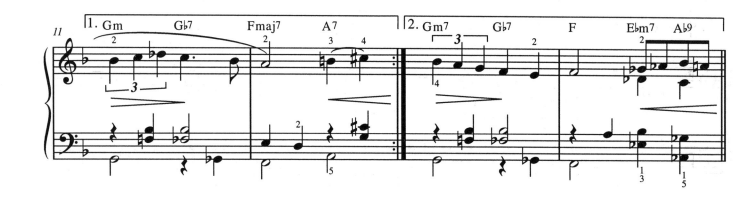

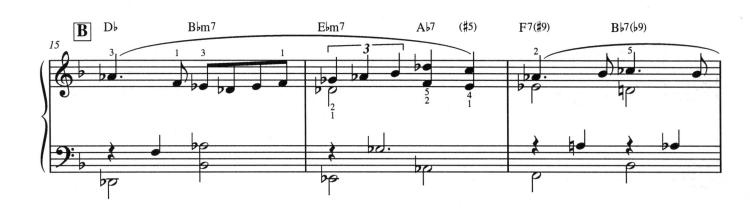

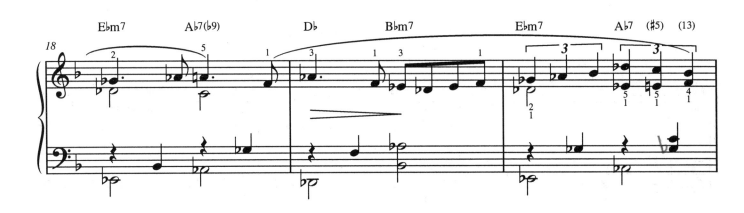

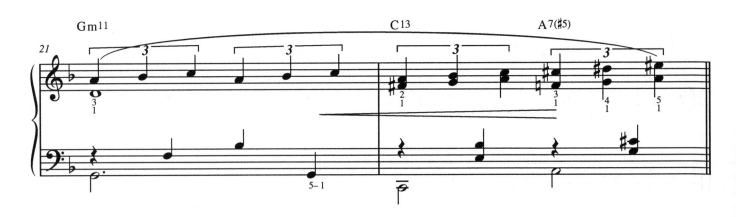

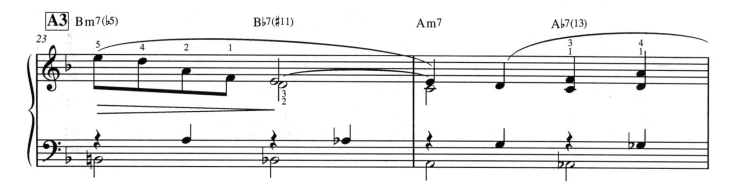

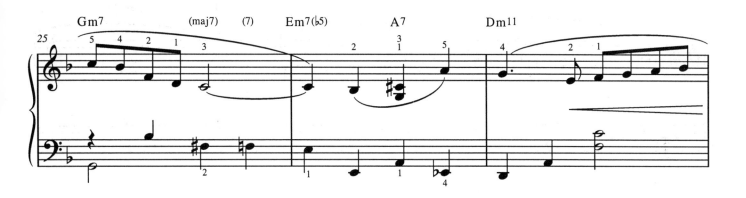

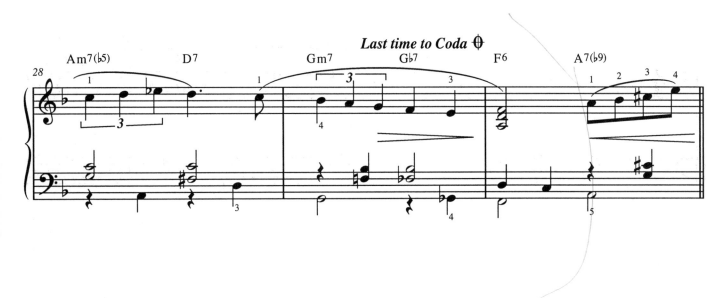

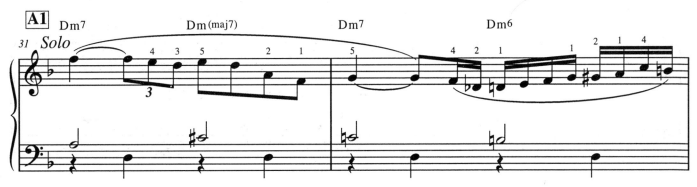

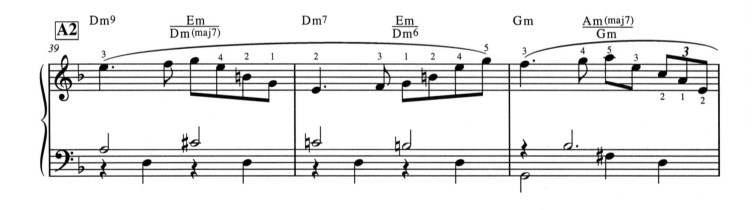

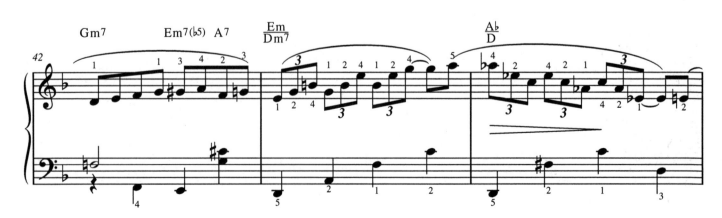

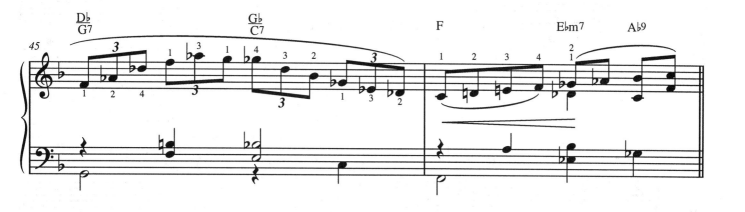

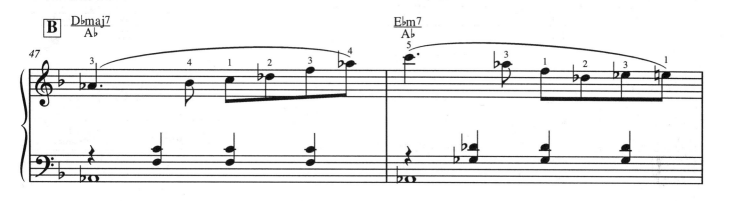

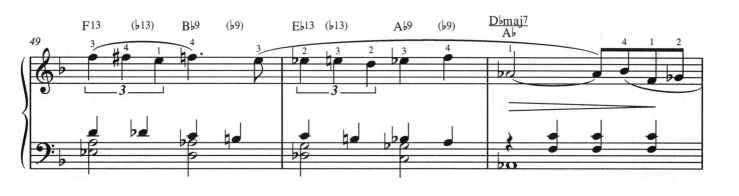

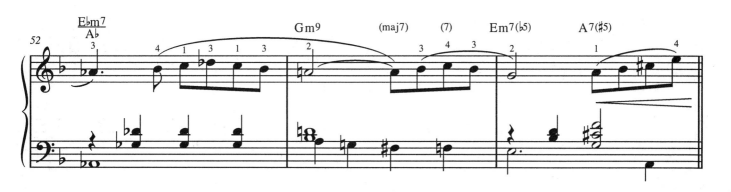

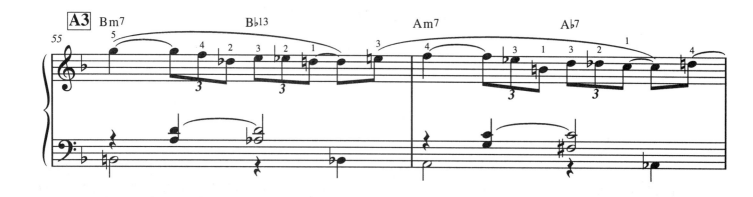

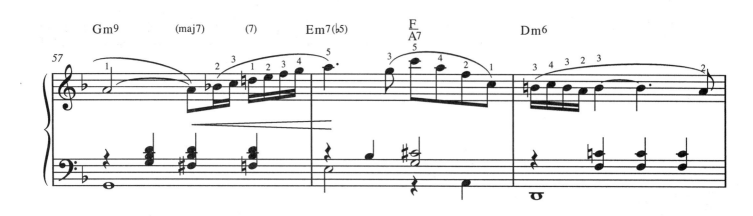

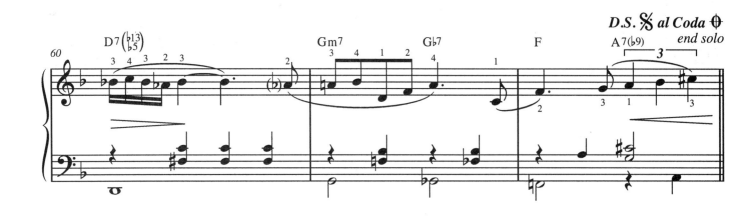

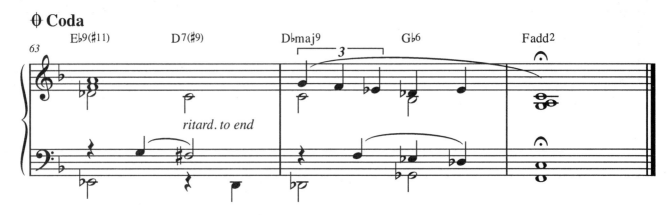

DANÇA VERÃO

Noreen Lienhard

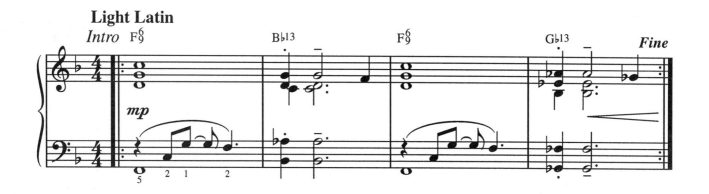

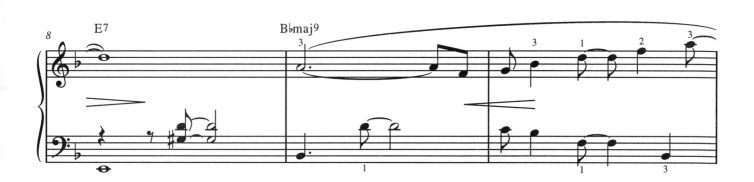

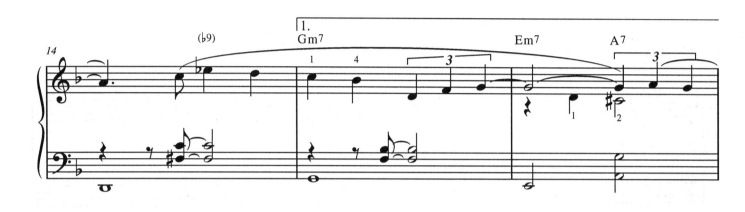

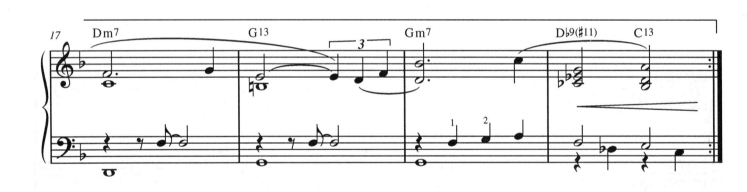

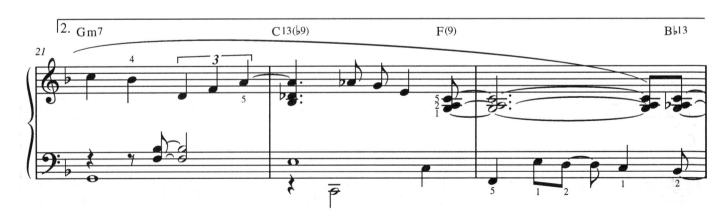

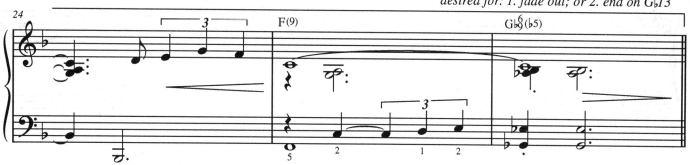

Last time jump to intro (mm. 1–4), repeat as desired for: 1. fade out; or 2. end on G♭13

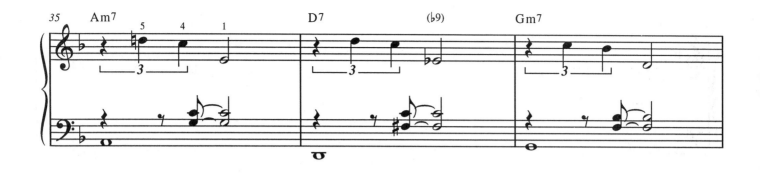

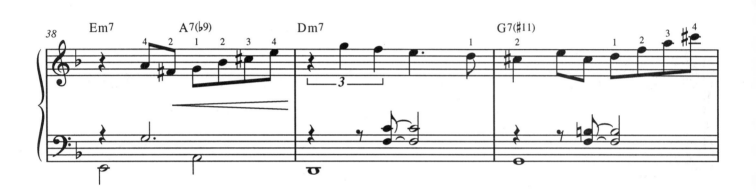

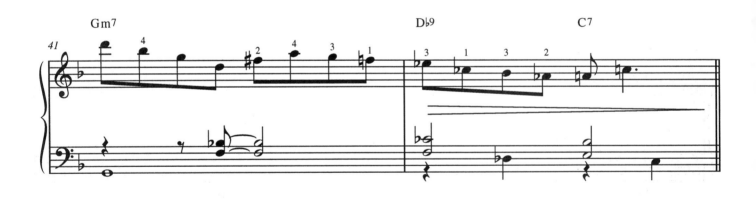

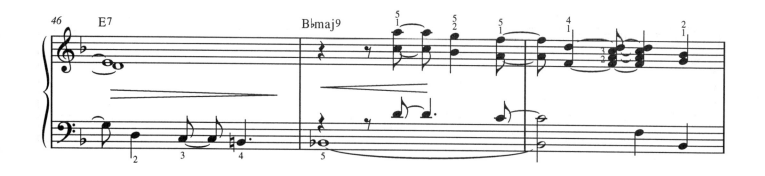

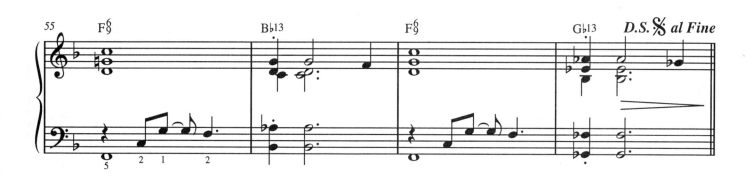

SEA AND SAND

Noreen Lienhard

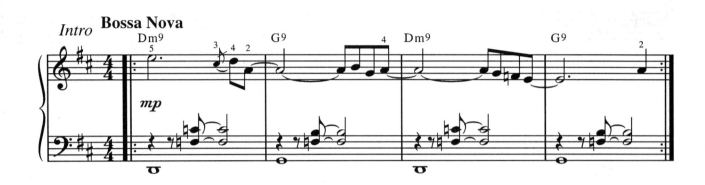

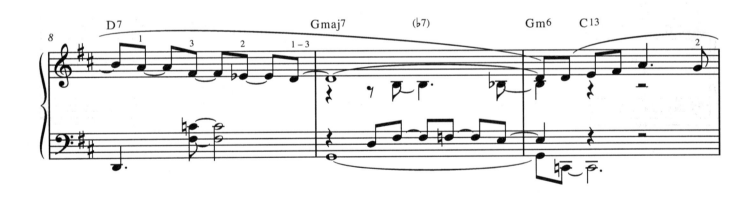

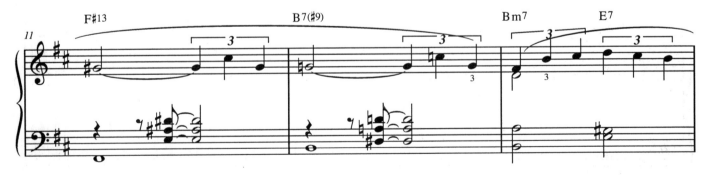

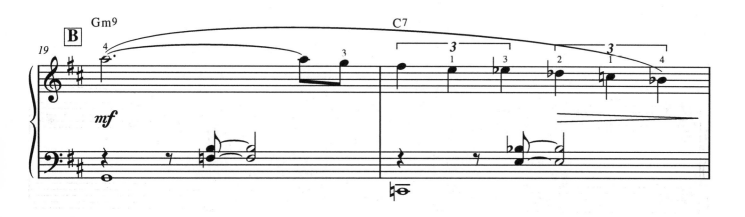

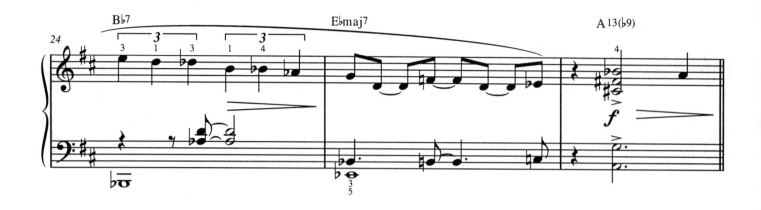

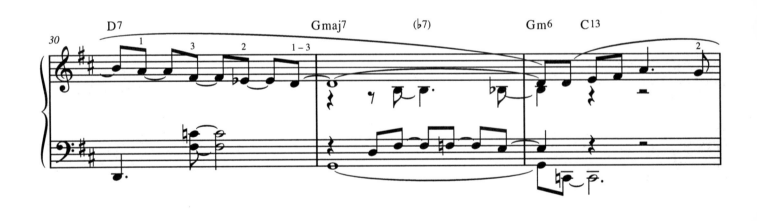

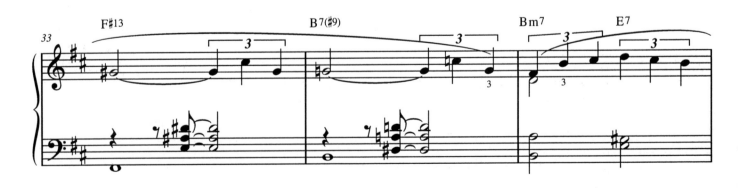

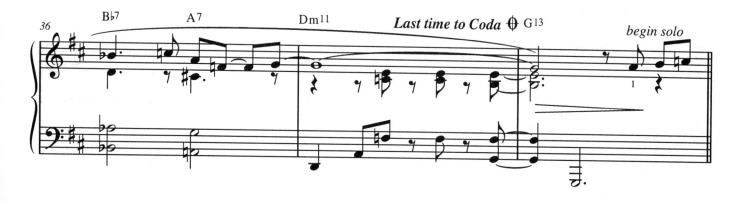

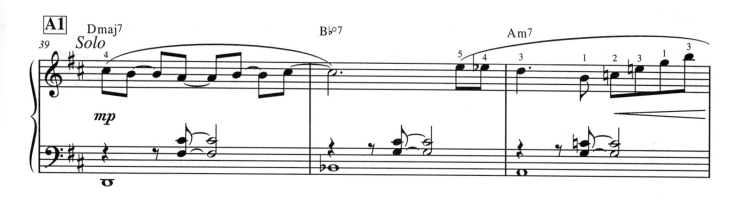

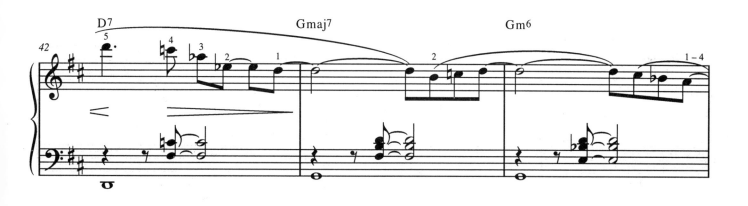

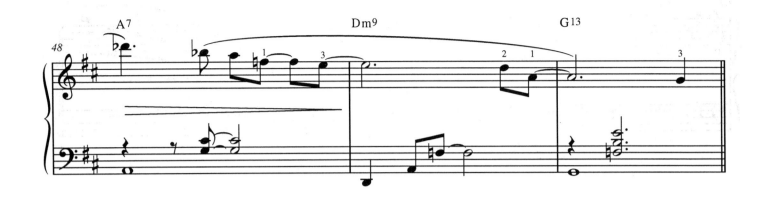

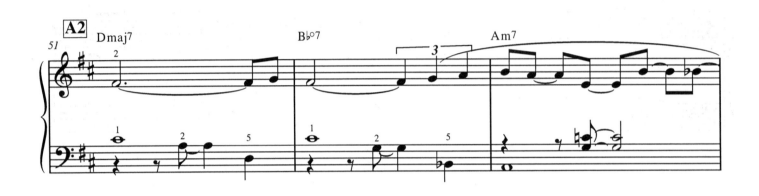

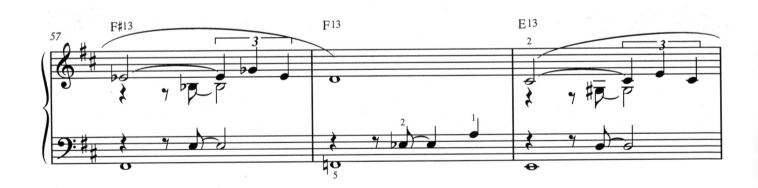

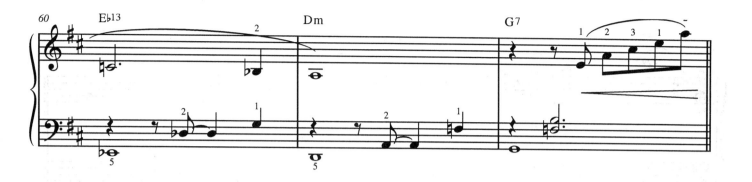

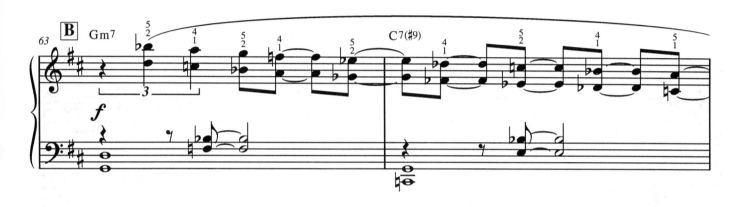

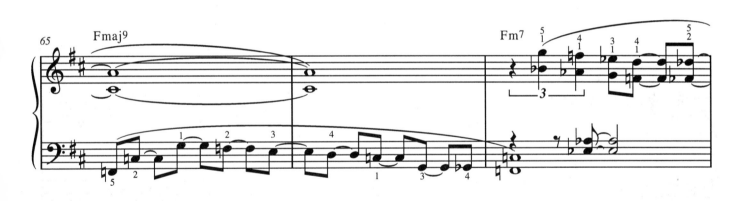

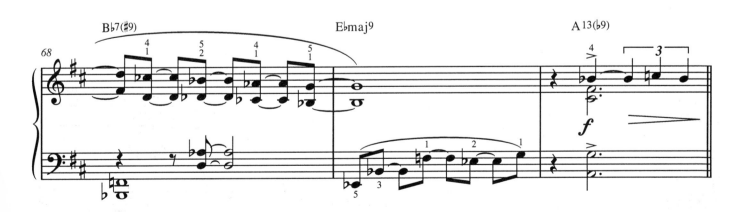

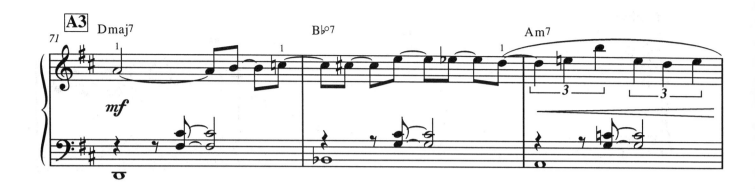

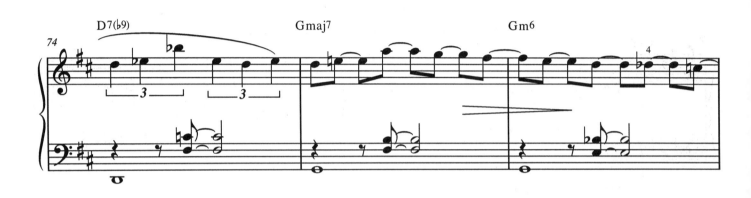

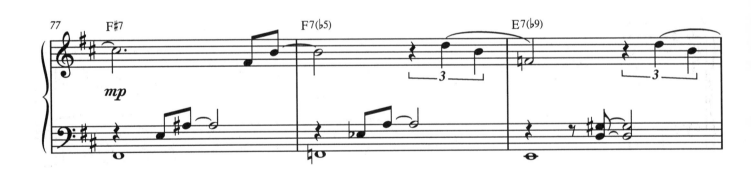

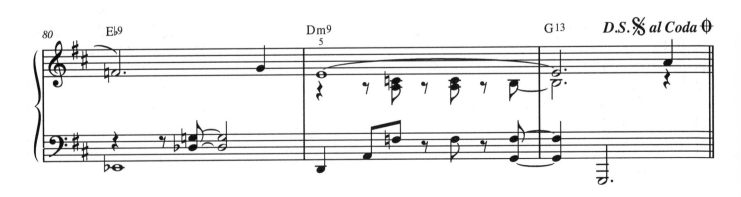

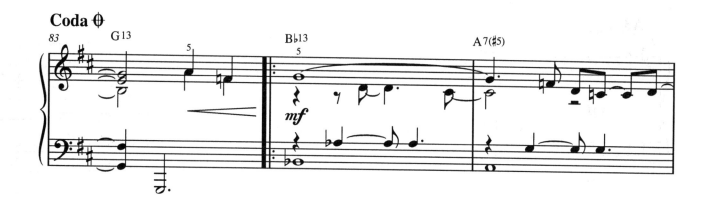

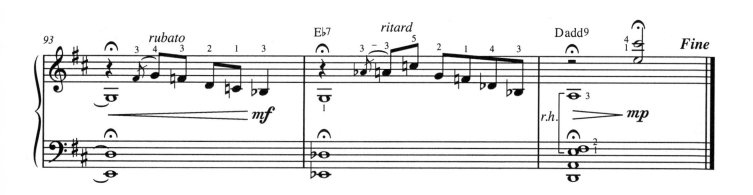

STARRY-EYED

Noreen Lienhard

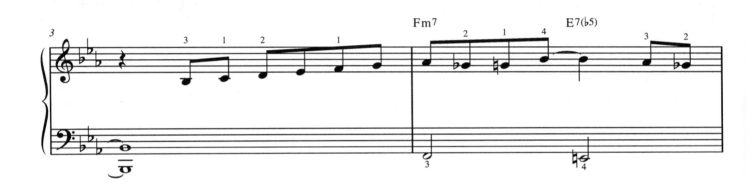

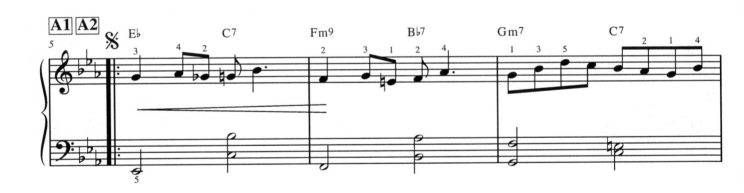

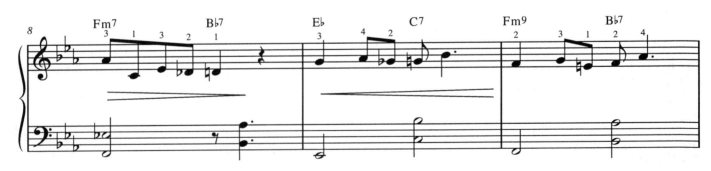

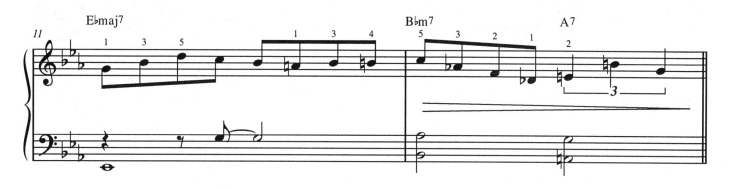

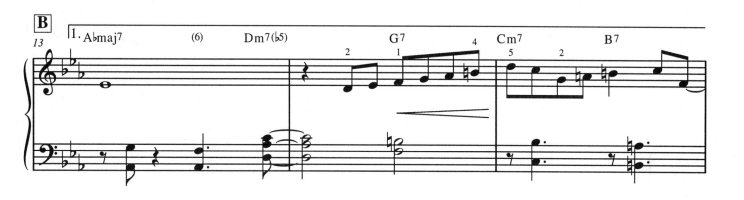

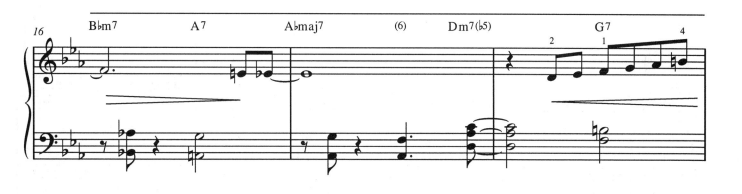

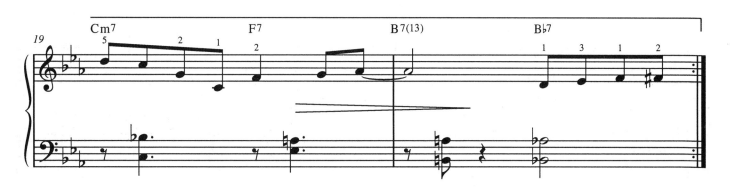

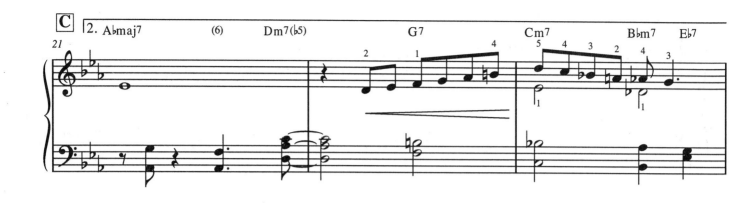

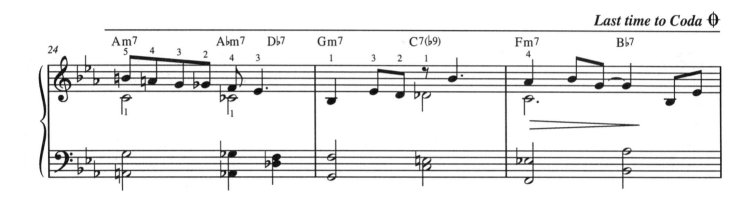

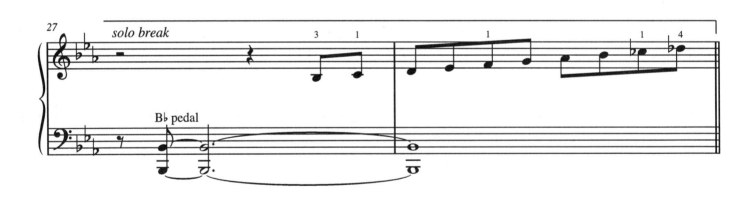

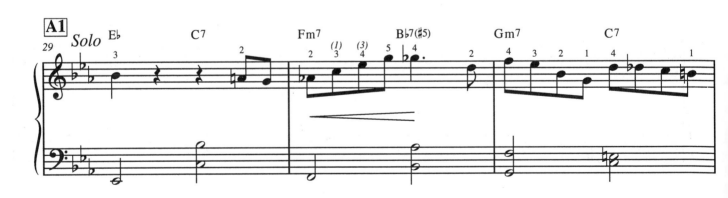

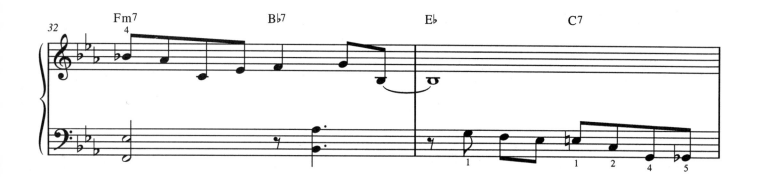

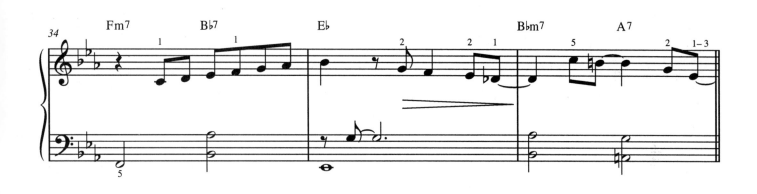

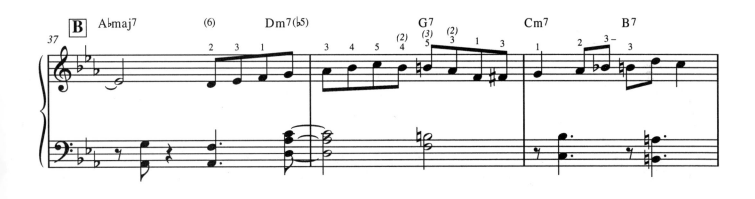

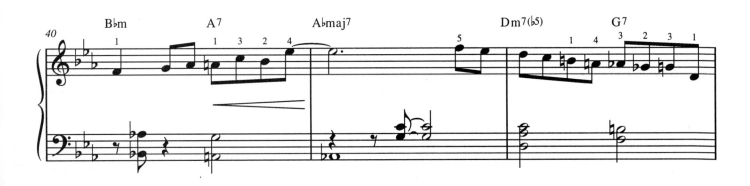

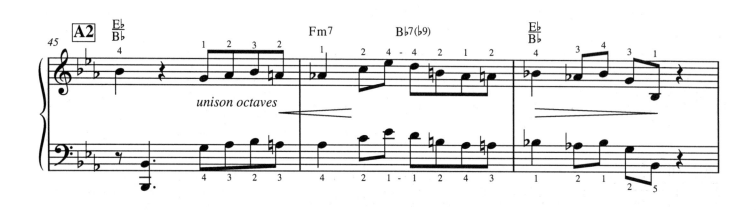

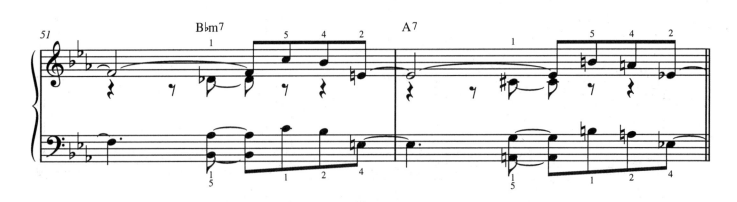

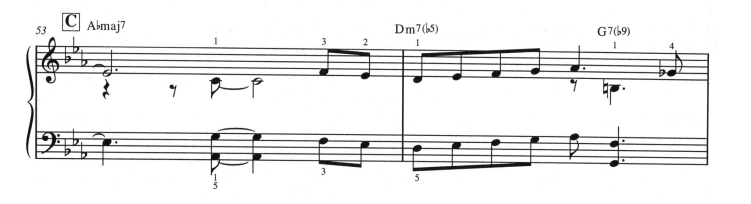

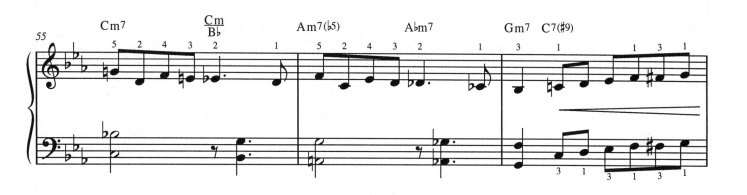

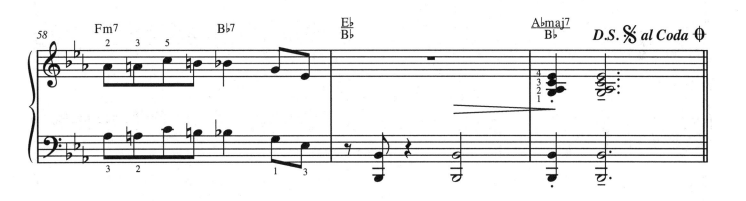

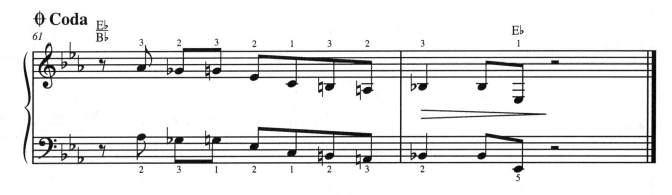

NIGHT WISHES

Noreen Lienhard

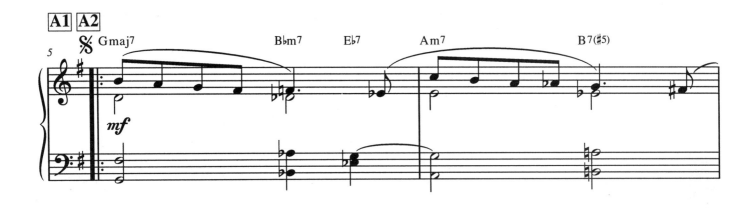

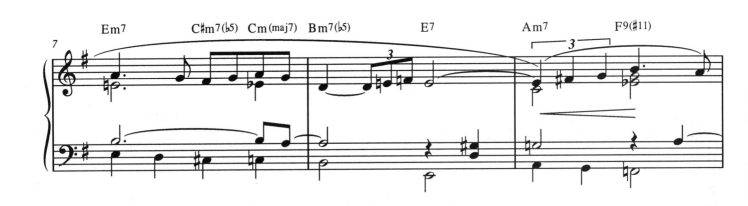

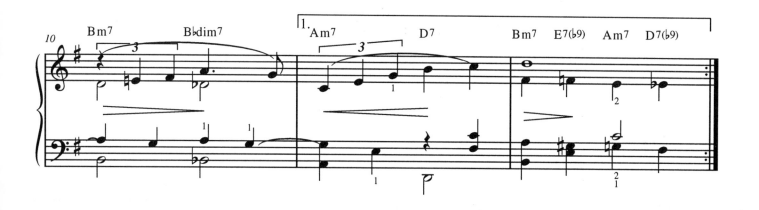

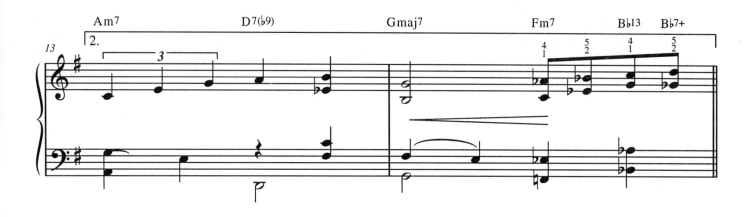

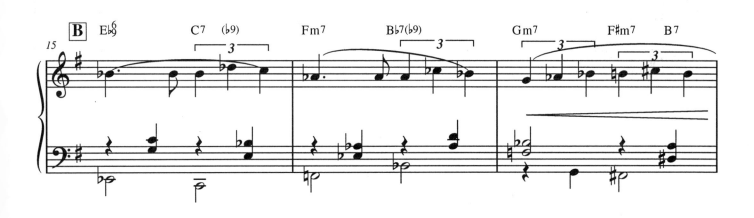

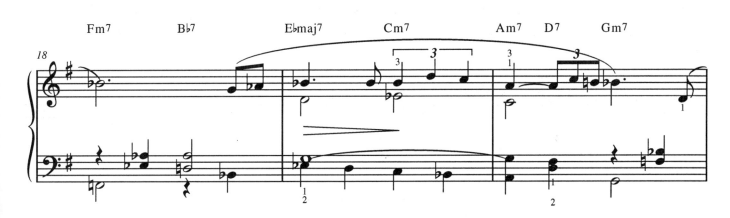

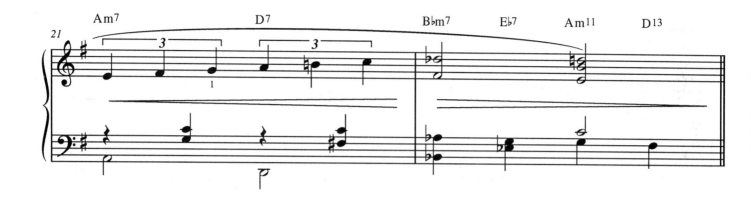

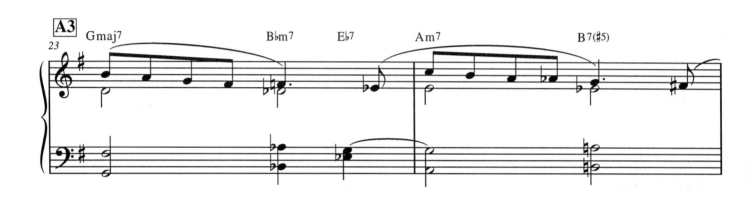

Last time to Coda ⊕

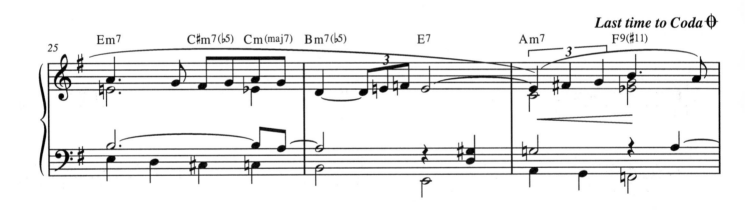

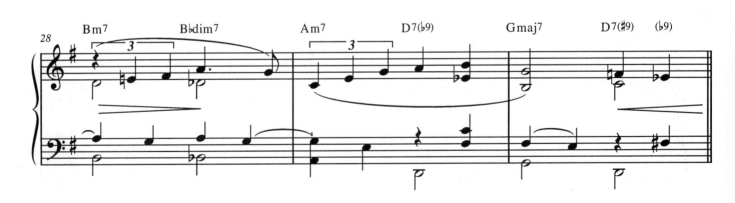

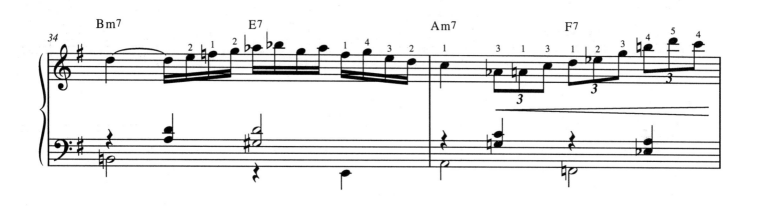

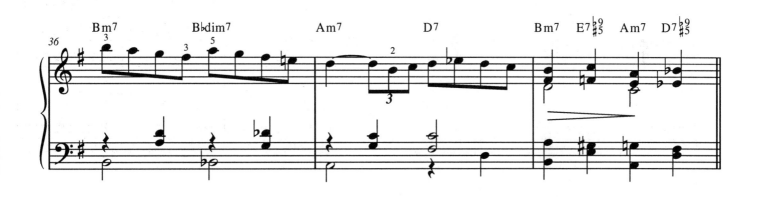

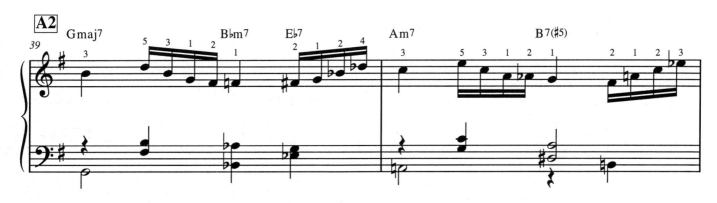

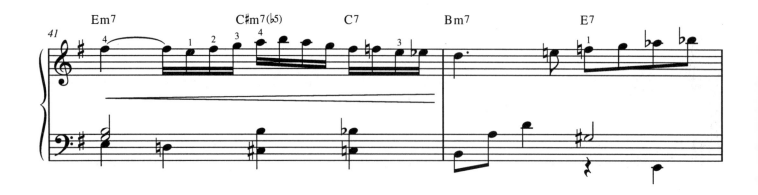

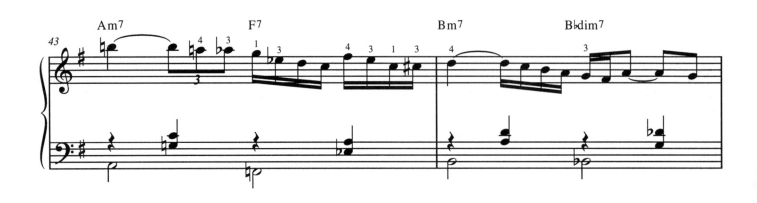

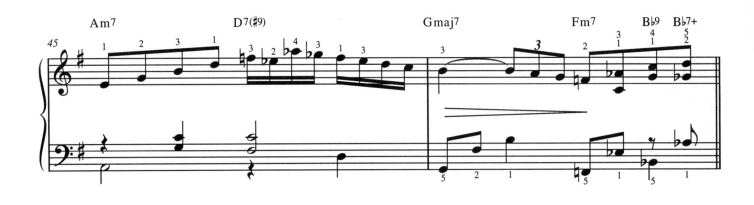

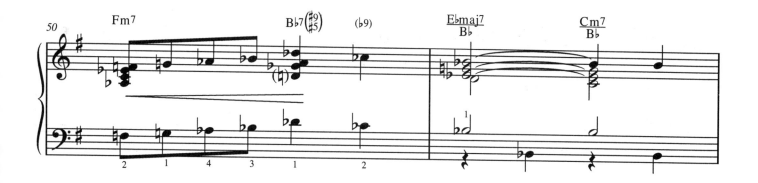

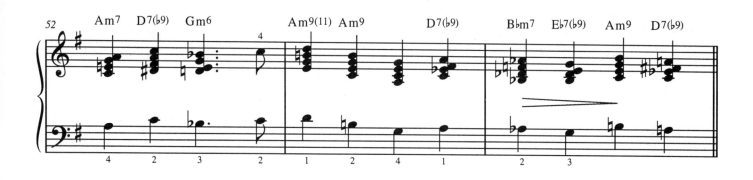

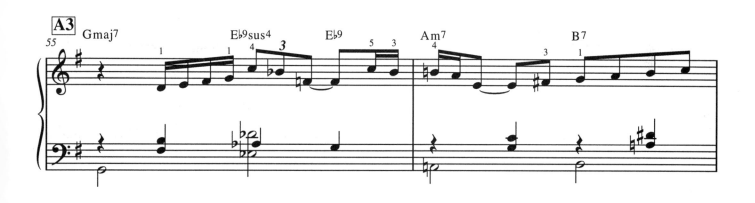

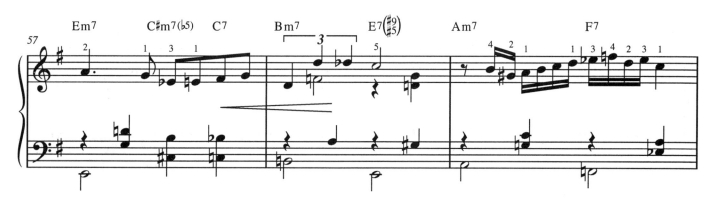

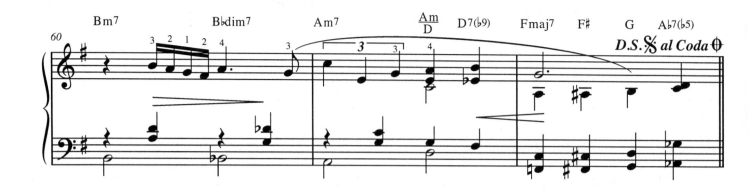

Coda ⊕

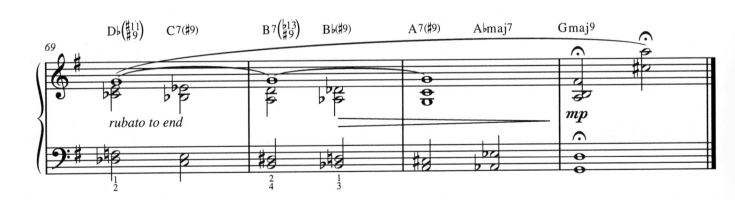

SURPRISE ENCOUNTER

Noreen Lienhard

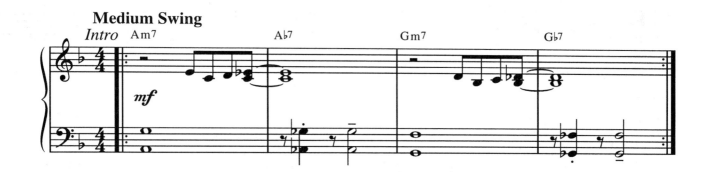

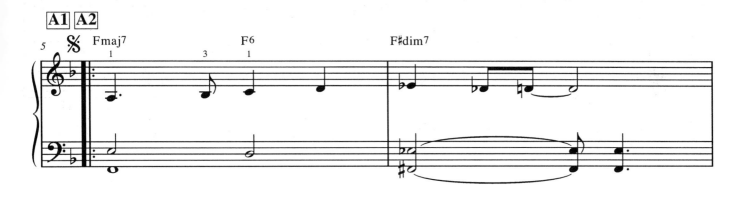

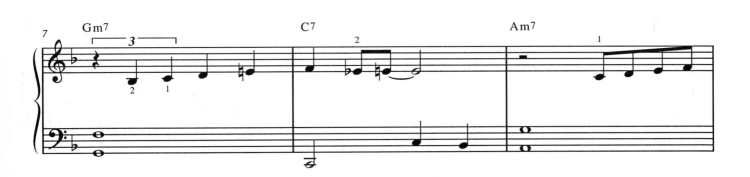

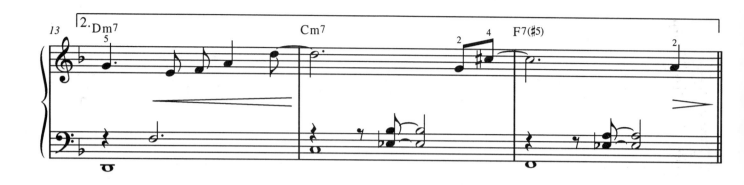

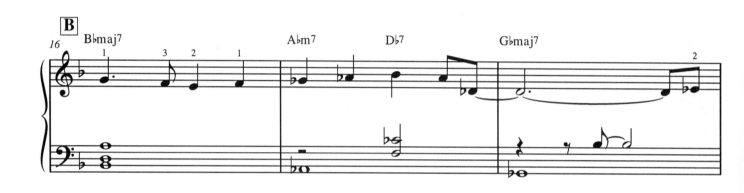

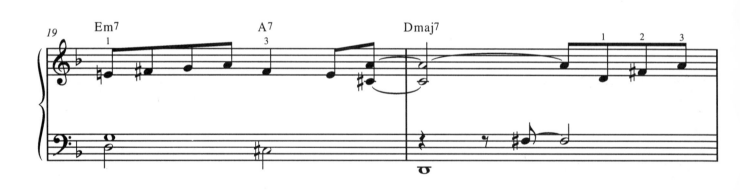

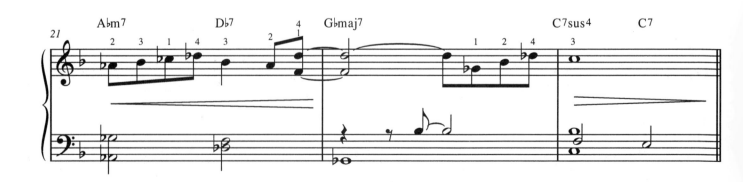

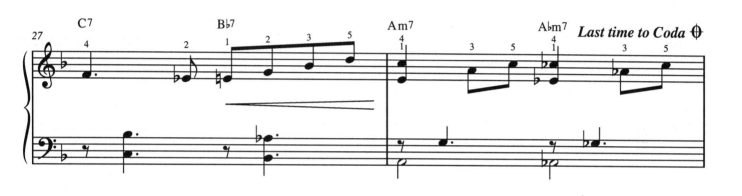

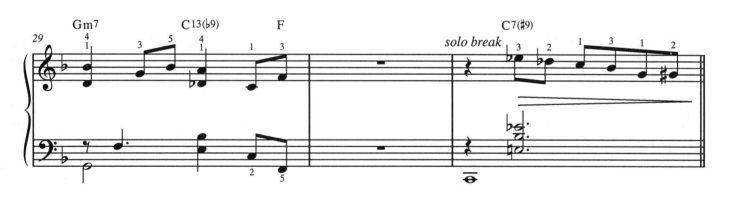

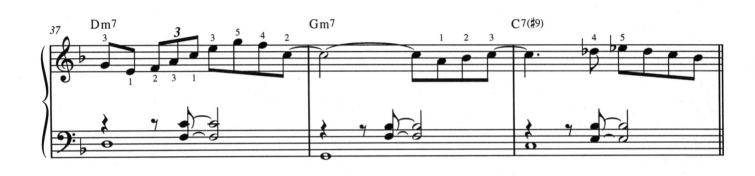

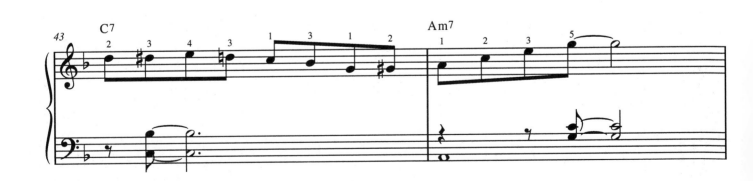

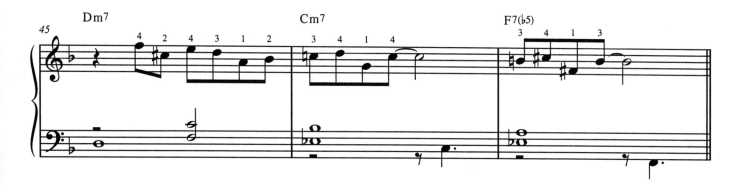

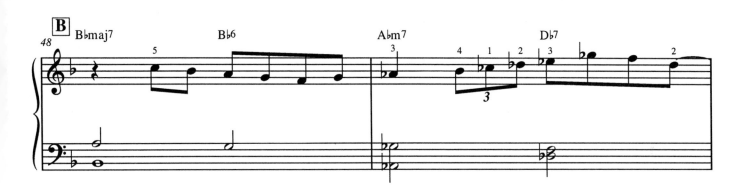

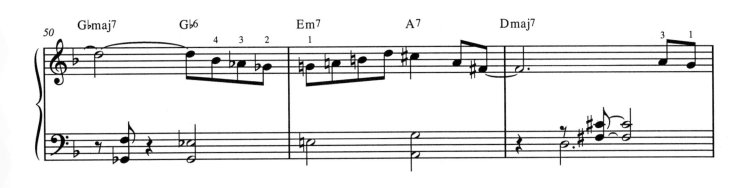

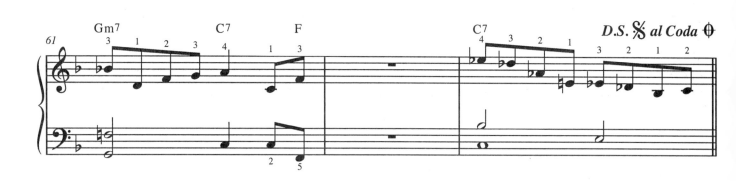

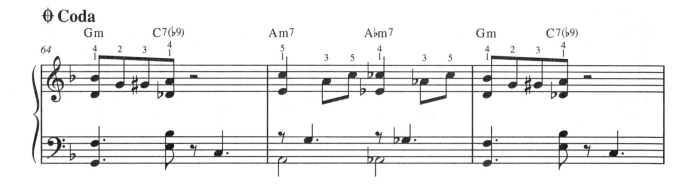

Coda

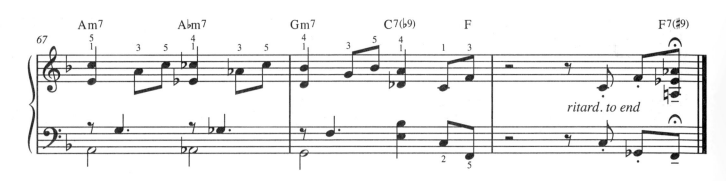

VINTAGE CHARM

Noreen Lienhard

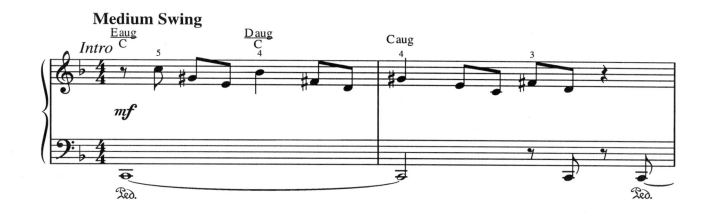

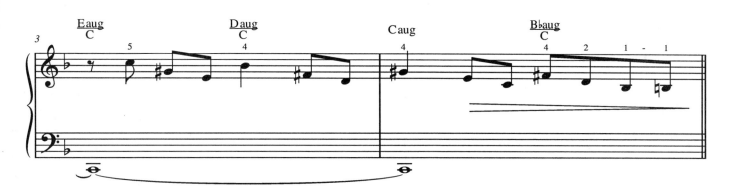

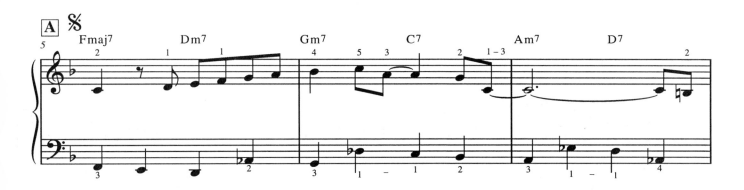

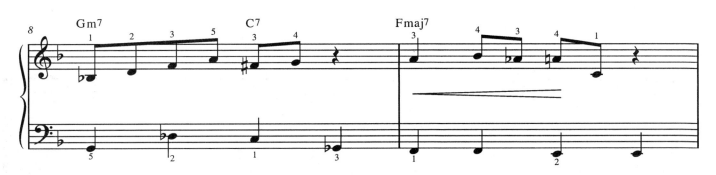

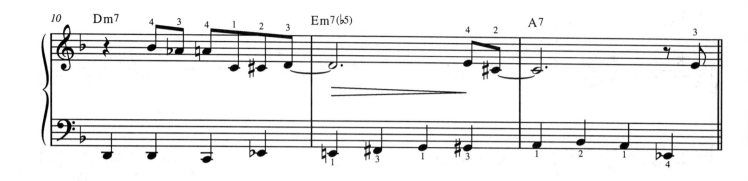

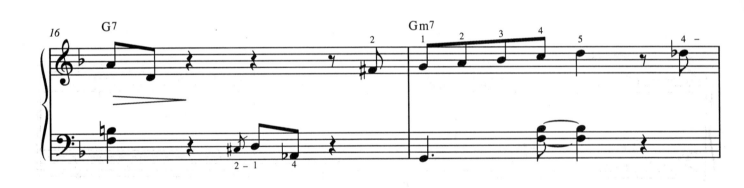

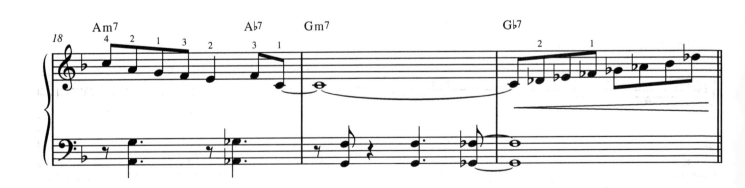

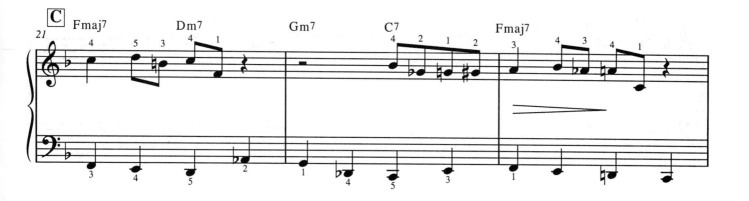

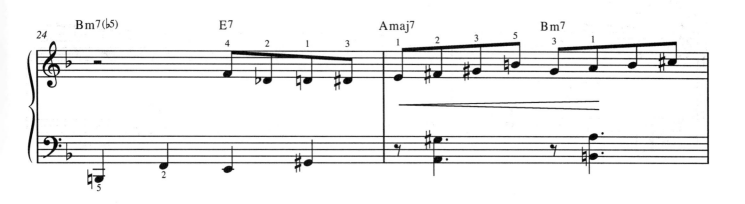

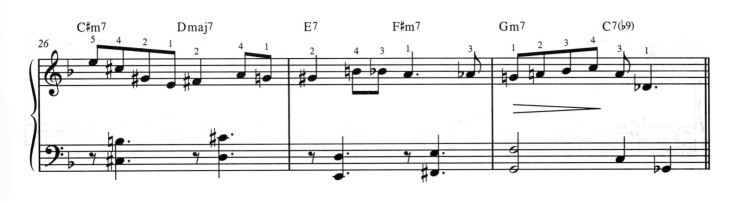

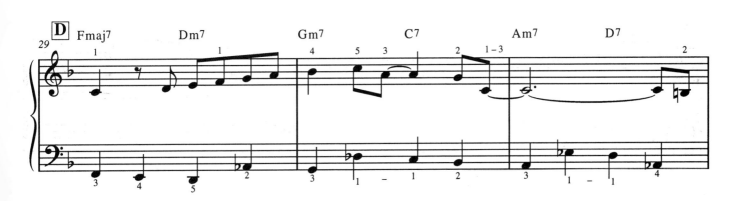

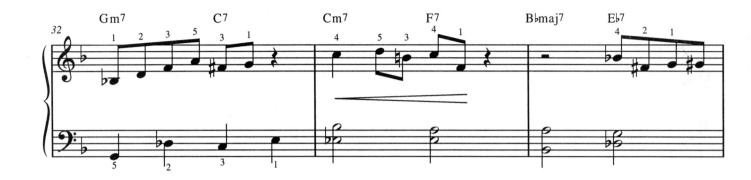

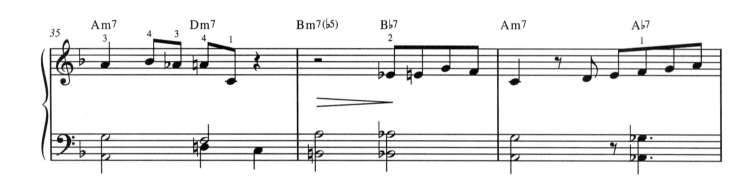

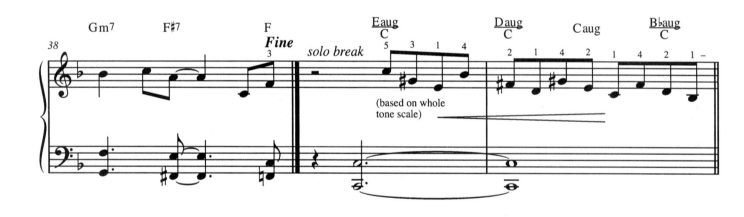

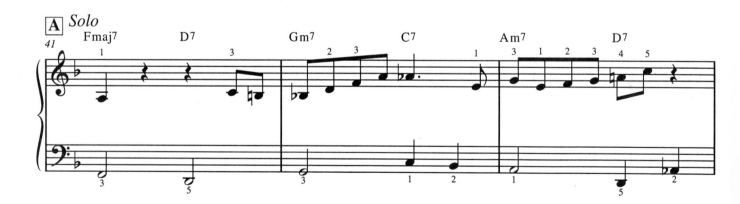

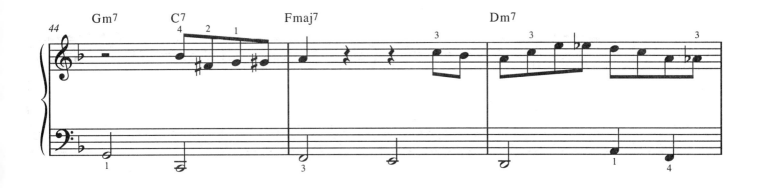

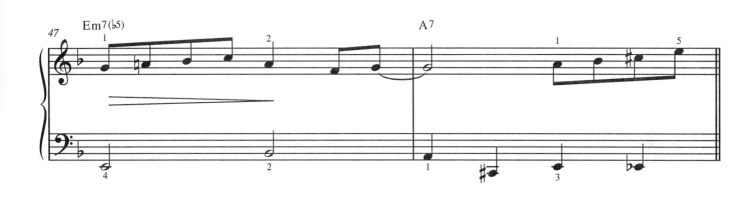

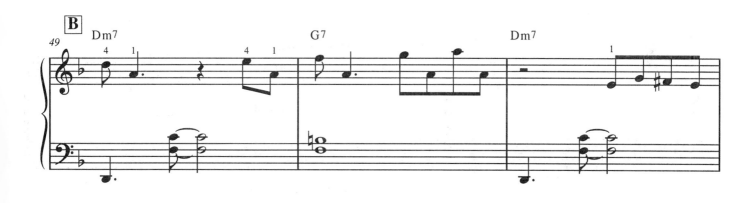

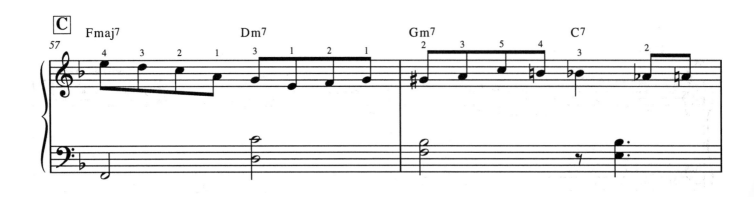

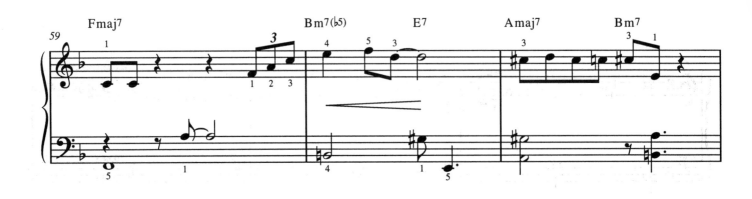

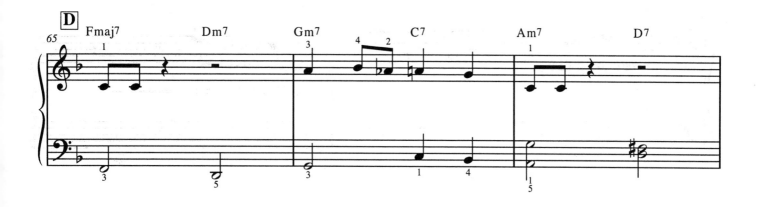

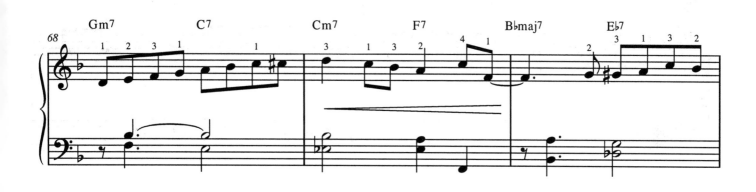

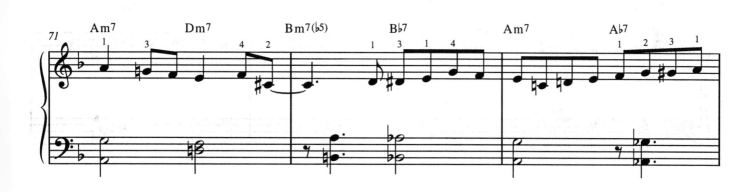

D.S. 𝄋 al Fine

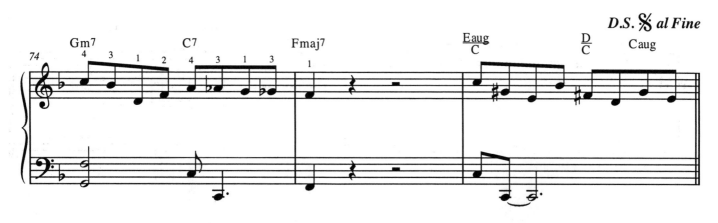

WAITING FOR MR. RIGHT

Noreen Lienhard

Jazz Waltz ♩ = 108

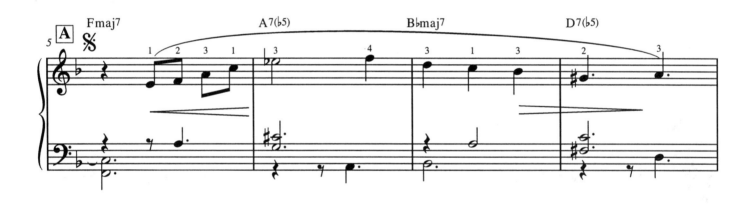

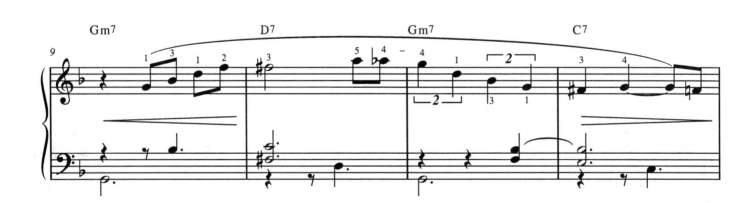

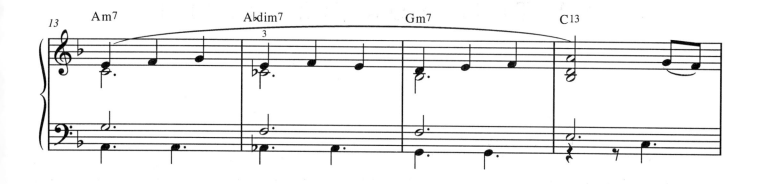

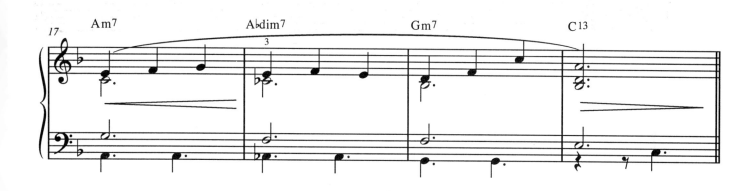

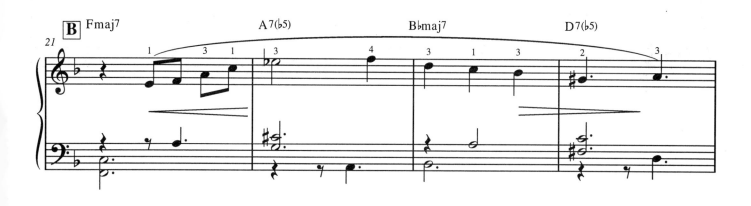

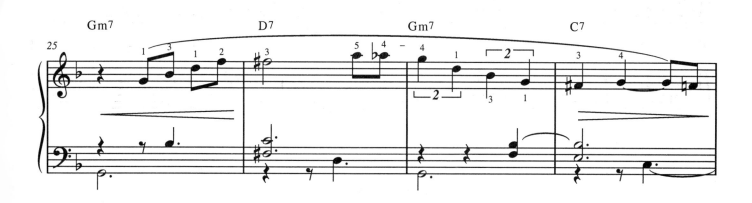

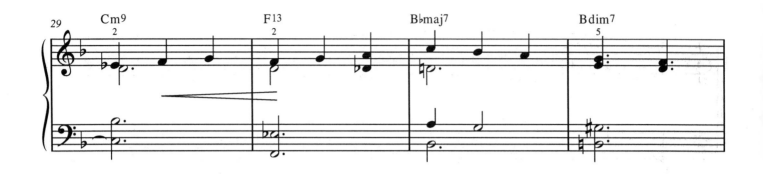

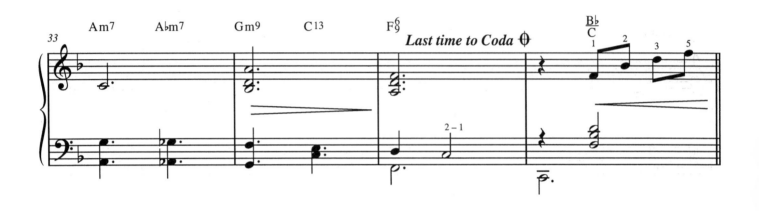

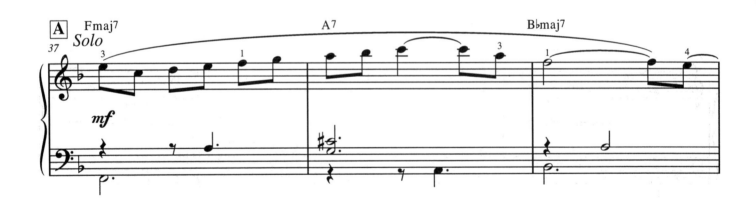

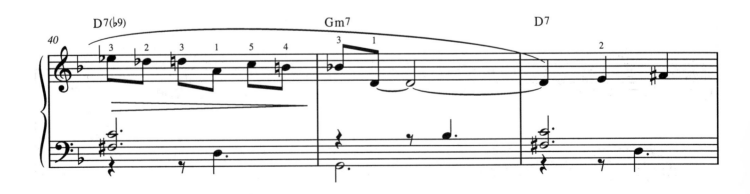

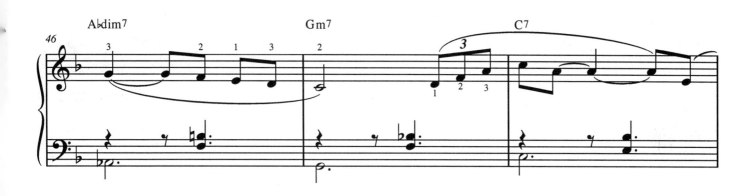

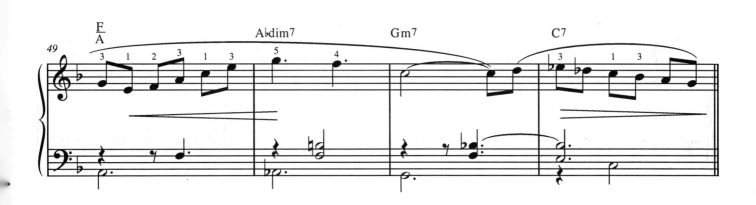

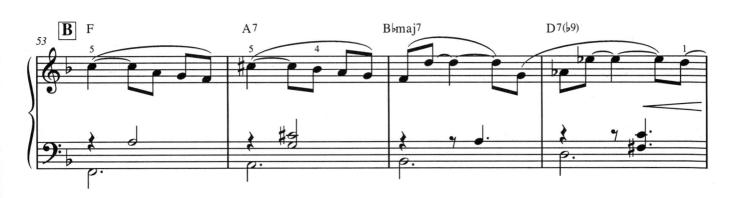

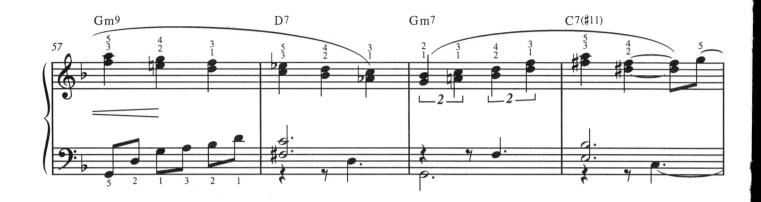

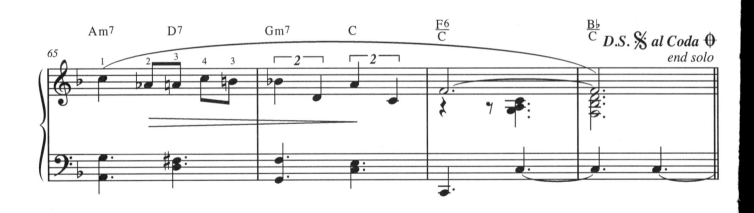

Repeat as desired for gradual fade-out ending.

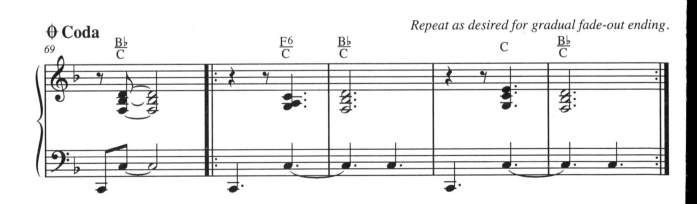

ABOUT THE AUTHOR

Noreen Lienhard is a contributing editor and arranger for both *Piano Today* magazine and *Sheet Music Magazine*. Her piano books, and books for which she has contributed piano renditions, including *It's Easy To Be Great*, *Professional Stylings for the Solo Pianist*, and *Keyboard Runs for the Pop & Jazz Stylist* are among the most sought-after on the market today. She has also contributed to many volumes in the Steinway Library of Piano Music series, *Piano Stylings of the Great Standards*, as well as a play-along collection of jazz improvisations on timeless standards that includes printed music and two CD recordings, entitled *Jazz Piano Play Along—You Plus A Jazz Ensemble*. A remarkable pianist, she has performed with such jazz luminaries as drummer Joe Morello, saxophonist Pepper Adams, trumpeters Howard McGhee and Clark Terry, and she can be heard on bassist Rufus Reid's CD, *Back To Front*. She has been featured on Marian McPartland's *Piano Jazz*, the National Public Radio show, and can be heard on the Christmas CD, *An NPR Jazz Christmas Vol. 2 – Marian McPartland and Friends*.